The Black Box of I

The Black Box of Her Dreams

Morteza Mohammadzadeh

CWP
Central West Publishing

This edition has been published by Central West Publishing, Australia
© 2024 Central West Publishing

All rights reserved. No part of this volume may be reproduced, copied, stored, or transmitted, in any form or by any means, electronic, photocopying, recording, or otherwise. Permission requests for reuse can be sent to editor@centralwestpublishing.com

For more information about the books published by Central West Publishing, please visit https://centralwestpublishing.com

Disclaimer
Every effort has been made by the publisher, editors and authors while preparing this book, however, no warranties are made regarding the accuracy and completeness of the content. The publisher, editors and authors disclaim without any limitation all warranties as well as any implied warranties about sales, along with fitness of the content for a particular purpose. Citation of any website and other information sources does not mean any endorsement from the publisher, editors and authors. For ascertaining the suitability of the contents contained herein for a particular lab or commercial use, consultation with the subject expert is needed. In addition, while using the information and methods contained herein, the practitioners and researchers need to be mindful for their own safety, along with the safety of others, including the professional parties and premises for whom they have professional responsibility. To the fullest extent of law, the publisher, editors and authors are not liable in all circumstances (special, incidental, and consequential) for any injury and/or damage to persons and property, along with any potential loss of profit and other commercial damages due to the use of any methods, products, guidelines, procedures contained in the material herein.

A catalogue record for this book is available from the National Library of Australia

ISBN (print): 978-1-922617-61-3

...and me in that cold winter
This is how I celebrated the birthday of my first white poem in the corner of the blackboard...
One day I will release my whole body and soul from this swamp...
By Dream Of a calm beach.
I will leap in the dark and wrestle with rocks of the river...

In the name of God

This flood of ink that poured to the paper was the result of every single thought and wish that
remained in my mind like a swamp and they had no way out.
The wishes and feelings that I had nurtured in my mind and heart for years...
Days passed and passed, a time arrived when day by day the pain of giving birth to thoughts and
words intensified in my mind and hurt my soul.
where the small constriction of life was squeezing my chest and made my heart beat slower and slower...
curtain of dust had been drawn over my heart.
Once I came to my senses and realized that my heart stopped beating and lost its nature, which is
full of love, kindness and happiness.
I desperately wanted to get out of the swamp that I had built for myself for years and flow, to be on
a path that is different from the previous years of my life.
I gave my heart to a path that I had no knowledge of
A path that I did not know the end of, and I was flowing alone because I could not believe the gradual
death of my heart and feelings.
A part of me was left in the middle of an endless road, and another part remained still and
motionless in the swamp of my imagination and belief...
The enthusiasm of the flow had taken over my whole being and seeing the other world made me ecstatic every moment.

A world that surprises you every moment and stops you from standing...

Walnut shakes your heart and creates a new growth in the veins and roots of your heart.

It fills your moments with love and happiness...

In the middle of the road that I was going, what rocks that broke my head, what trees that blocked

my way, and what holes that filled with my soul, I flowed...

The holes that had dried up in the corner of my heart and mind for several years...

I am like a river with no destination that has no end...

Only an infinite force pushed me to continue, gave me branches and leaves and made me more productive...

The continuation of the road that ends at the sea.

I did not know about that endless sea

A sea of love and feeling and kindness

The sea where thousands of rivers had met, a river from the heart of the forest, a river from the

heart of the desert, and a river that had split the rocks and reached there, would forever calm me down.

We had come to the conclusion that the wishes of all human beings had been fulfilled there, without

any indication of their class, without any question of where you came from and who you are...

There, only love commanded, the love that beats in the hearts of all people

The love that made us consider all that is a part of us and give it love and kindness...
The embrace of the sea was open to all the rivers that flowed towards it and it accepted them
wholeheartedly without knowing what gender, skin or ethnicity you are, it dissolved us all in itself
without any difference...
And that huge sea always had a long-standing expectation in its heart, waiting for the swamps left
in the corner of this world that had no way to flow and had forgotten the desire to flow, and they
had fallen into a deep slumber, unaware that a huge sea full of peace and purity was waiting for them.
My hands are the author of this story and I am the supervisor of these writings...
Like a drop that wants to tell about the boundless sea
From the sea that one day embraced me and gave me life
Maybe he is writing for a piece of me in that swamp, and maybe a piece of me that is still hurting
somewhere far away wants to heal its pain and also...
I hammer my pen like a nail into the concrete wall of that swamp of beliefs that has held us captive
for years and writes in the hope of an opening to free our whole being and flow to a path whose end is
nothing but the sea, unity and love.

..

"The beginning of the story"
The sun was slowly rising...
The sun had sprinkled golden and yellow color in the corner of the sky...
The cold morning breeze appeared in the city and stole the sleep from people's eyes...
That morning was not like the previous days for me
As if someone else woke up instead of me.
I woke up earlier than usual.
My whole look and thoughts were different
I could see the color of the light in the sky
Or hear the pleasant sound of my feet kissing the ground
Until yesterday, when I had reached the age of 28 and a few months,
I had not been able to see the
greatness and beauty of the sun in that way, or to touch the wind
that hits my face to the marrow of my bones.
In these last days, life has become very slow for me
The days came and passed by, I had no enthusiasm left, to endure
the masks that people put on them
faces out of necessity and to make ends meet is more painful than
the mask that you have to put on
all day long. bring to the night
Repetitive tasks and predetermined circular life bothered me.
Maybe decaying in everyday life, enduring the stress and worries of
the work environment, as well as

the drying of the roots of love and happiness in my being, had forced me to wake up before the sun rose and move to nowhere, I wanted to run alone. I should take a walk from whatever it is until no one has woken up and the sounds of factories and machines and their restrictions have not started.

I should go to the corner of the city and take a walk so that maybe I can have a few minutes to myself and spend time with myself.

For several years, my legs were moaning from bearing the heavy weight on his shoulders, and these days he didn't want to take me anywhere anymore.

That day, because of my legs, which I had promised to exercise, I was walking to lose weight and take the burden off their shoulders...

I walked for a few minutes at a slow pace, I couldn't catch my breath and my whole face was soaked with sweat, all my thoughts and mind were turned off, and at the moment I was catching my breath, slowly, a new feeling had formed in my whole body and soul. And the more tired I got, the more I felt happy, joyful, and alive. After I walked for half an hour on a beautiful green path, I realized that I was far away from the city.

I had almost reached the corners of it; I was stressed that I might not be able to reach my work at

the specified time and receive a warning about this.
To return, I had to travel a long way to get home, of course, if there is a way back for me

I looked at the clock and changed my direction towards home

Slowly and with measured steps, I passed by a large garden, the grandeur and beauty of which attracted the eyes of every passerby.

My head was high and I was staring at the clean buildings and trees.

I was excited as if I had never seen such a scene before

And I was full of excitement

I was enjoying looking at all the beautiful nature and the area that was nothing less than the

paradise that had been described to us for years.

Indeed, that area was the paradise

It was the best place I could ever see

I didn't feel time, the only real experience was the moments I had with me...

Think of it, spending several years of your life moving between specific lines and doing repetitive and

determined tasks every day, and spending all the years of your life in a certain and predetermined path that you may not have chosen yourself.

And suddenly a force takes you away from the path you have made for yourself for years and leads you astray.

And make your heart beat again

From afar, I saw a man in a neat and stylish black suit coming towards me, he came closer and stood in front of me:

Hello

Sir, who are you working with?

Who are you?

What are you doing here this morning?

It took me a few moments to get myself out of that atmosphere and its beautiful nature, when I came to myself

I said to him with a smile:

I was actually walking...

I moved a little away from the city and the beautiful view here drew me here, I had nothing to do

with anyone, it's a shame.

And I had just come to exercise for a few minutes

I have to go home now.

Ignoring my words, he nodded

He was guiding me to the way I should return from there...

Please come back this way, this is not a private area or a place for walking

You have come the wrong way

When he said this, I lowered my head and was disappointed

I made my way home to go back

For a moment, a distant voice caught the attention of me and the guard:

A little on the other side, a soft voice said:

Tell the guard to come inside, he has something to do with me.

We both turned and saw an old man on the other side of the trees with his head down.

Sir, they have come the wrong way, I told them to go back

There is nothing wrong, please guide them to come inside

The guard said: yes sir, I am now telling them to come to you...

The guard looked at me with surprised eyes and said, "I'm sorry sir, I didn't recognize you. I'm sorry."

You must be the special guest who was supposed to meet the boss today

And I didn't think you would come at this hour of the day.

To my surprise, I wanted to say that I neither know you nor the owner of this property and palace.

We were both surprised

I got a strange feeling...

I wanted to say that I have nothing to do with anyone and I just came here to walk

The guard guided me inside with his hands and said, please ...

I couldn't speak, I couldn't say anything, as if someone had really invited me and everyone was waiting for me to come.

My legs moved forward involuntarily

We entered a garden through a large door

The wet sweat on my face and forehead was getting colder and colder...

I did not know anyone there

That old man must have mistaken me...

I didn't date anyone at all

It is here in this magnificent and beautiful garden

I have spent my whole day at work and at home, and at night I lay
my head on the pillow thinking
about tomorrow and what I have to do...
With these images passing through my mind, we were passing
through a narrow path surrounded by
flowers and green trees.
The distance between us and the old man seemed like a year had
passed before we left. Its moments
were so sweet and full of joy that I didn't want to lose a moment of
that time. All my senses and
thoughts were focused on the present.
An old man with a thin back and white beard was sitting on a
broken table next to a pond. You
couldn't understand what he was doing. When we got closer to him,
I just wanted him to look at me
and make sure that there was a mistake and he was going to kick me
out, but he didn't even look at
me. He didn't do it to me.
He was holding some small pebbles in his hand and was turning
them in his hands and looking at them...
The guard left me a few steps away from the old man and left...
I forced my tongue and greeted and said that sir, I think I
accidentally entered your garden and I
really had nothing to do here and an appointment with someone did
not bring me here.
I am very sorry to disturb you.

The old man raised his head and looked at me, a small smile appeared on his lips and again he put his head on the rocks.
and call the guard to take me away from there
But after a few moments he said: My son
Nothing in the world happens by chance and by mistake, and all events are according to special will
Even the movement of an ant in the most unknown region of the world is done for a purpose and to show purpose...
I was taken aback by his words for a moment
I didn't know the meaning of what he said and I didn't know the purpose of what happened and for what purpose I am here.
In order to get a clear answer from that old man, I showed myself firmly and seriously and said in a loud tone
Sir, what can I say, as I said, my legs have not been helping me for some time and the doctor told me?
that I must walk and exercise...
On the other hand, I am too busy with work and problems that I can't spend even a minute for myself
To be honest, the color and face of happiness, love and kindness has filled our lives and we are hard hit.
And to save myself from everyday life and repetition of boring events
And to get away from that repetitive and boring life. Even now, when I look at the clock, I see that I

am very late and I have to go back to work so that I don't have any problems.

I don't know you and I won't take up more of your time. It's a shame. If I came across your area, it was completely accidental.

I had gone this way unknown.

I said these words to the old man and saved myself.

But deep down I wanted to talk to that old man

His eyes were calm and motionless, like the sea that no stone could take its calmness away...

He gave me a meaningful look and stretched his hand towards me, he said, "Take my hand so that I can stand up."

When he got up, I could understand that he didn't need my help. He got up and told me that there was

no need to apologize. He said this and moved to walls a direction and wanted me to follow him.

I wanted to say that I am late and I have to go back

He said, didn't you come for a walk?

I said yes but...

He smiled and said, follow me

I reluctantly walked behind him

I matched my steps with the rhythm of his steps

I didn't want to think about anything except that moment.

I had a familiar feeling in a strange place

It is as if after several years you have returned to the house where you lived many years ago and everything is familiar to you, a feeling full of excitement and surprise but vague.

The old man was talking:

And I moved closer to him to hear his words:

This is the place where I spend my whole day

Every day I make a small part of this garden and live with its flowers, trees and rivers

These flowers and trees love me profoundly and I love each and every one of them

From its stones to the colors of its leaves in all seasons

From its insects to old trees that no longer give me fruit

Each one gives me a new breath

My soul and soul are tied to the roots of these plants and flowers and they give birth to me and give me life every day.

All those things that are here have souls and are connected with humans.

He looked up and showed the sun that came from behind the mountain and said that the sun that is above us with its greatness gives life to all these gardens and makes them bigger and bigger and for him grass and Flowers and plants are no different, because he knows that all that is here is the completion of a cycle and a puzzle.

I was listening and my head was down.

Before he talked about the sun, I was looking at the greatness of the sun at the beginning of me

walk, and now he is also talking about it.
What was going to happen? It's like a mystery is about to be unraveled for me!!
My ears were excited by all these different words, and I wanted to understand his words, and on the
other hand, my thoughts of many years were pulling me towards the same direction.
In complete surprise, I opened my mouth to speak with a trembling voice
I wished him good health and said that in the midst of this rush of hustle and bustle and everyday
hardships, here is like a pleasant paradise for a person. Good for you that this garden is big and more
importantly, you have a big and kind heart.
And I never thought about what you said, but it was sweet for me
He was walking without paying attention to my words
I could feel that my words are like a pebble thrown into the sea, so small compared to all the depth.
As if my words failed to reach his ears and he didn't pay attention to it
He looked at a point in front of him and walked calmly and confidently...
He told me:
You are familiar to me, and I have seen you in a moment of my life that I have never forgotten that

scene and your image, and I remember that we had a good relationship and you made me feel myself again.

Just when my life needed it to happen.

I thought, no matter how much I looked at my past, I couldn't remember anything

I could not remember him, I had never seen him

No, no, I have never seen such a person in my life...

But there was a strange feeling for me, like being thrown from a small strait into a big and raging

river, I was so lost, all the events were new to me.

My breath was getting fresh and I could communicate with all the trees and flowers and even the tables and benches.

I didn't stay locked in my thoughts for a moment and watched everything I saw and felt.

I told him, I don't know, maybe we met each other at work, I deal with different people every day.

Unfortunately, I don't have enough memory to remember all of them

He looked at me and said no with a small grin on his face

You have not seen me in your workplace

He said this and sat on a yellow bench next to a bush and I sat on the other side of the bench. I had

forgotten everything.

Going to work, coming home, my to-do list

All these thoughts jumped out of my head

I said, if it's possible, tell me how you know me, I haven't seen you
until now or I don't remember, and I
passed by here a long time before I reached your garden...
He said: As I said, nothing happens by chance, I have been waiting
for you for a long time, there are a
series of things that I have to share with you, maybe I have fulfilled
a little of my mission.
And maybe I was blind to the bright side for you on the road ahead
of you
I was very curious to find out about this incident and to hear and
understand the vague and unknown
words of that old man.
I wanted to ask the question that arose in my mind every moment
He continued:
I was drowned several years ago.
And my heart stopped beating
And he wanted to stop hitting me forever
It was the end of my life as if you were a few steps away from the
precipice of death and you had no
choice but to jumping, jumping with clipped wings.
And someone like you will come from astray and remind me to
jump
You opened my wings; you gave me my flying feather again and I
experienced flight instead of falling
and dying in that abyss.
If you didn't come, I would never feel alive again...

I thought a little and no matter how much I looked back, I had not saved anyone from drowning

In order to make the matter clear to me

I immediately asked him with a confused face, can I ask where you drowned, which river or sea?

Which direction?

He said no, there was no river or sea, by the way, on the contrary

I was drowned on land and you rescued me from that land and threw me into the sea...

An endless sea that is the resting place of all human beings.

A sea that I did not know existed

His words make me think more and more and reach the deepest layer of my being

I always had unheard and unsaid words deep inside me, which became more prominent in me recently,

now it was as if he was calling from the depths of my heart...

He said the same words that I felt had been in the depths of my mind and heart for years and I had

never been able to live them.

His words were like a handkerchief that was stretched over the dusty mirror of my heart and showed

me more clearly to myself...

His voice was familiar to my heart

I said:

Tell me more about which land are you talking about??

Which sea??

Which flight???

With a calm tone in his voice

And with staring eyes

Without even blinking and noticing anything around him, he told

me the whole story:

It was the middle of February

I was spending time at school

I woke up half-heartedly at 7 in the morning...

I had put a paper wrapper behind its battery so that it wouldn't turn

off and it could wake me up

first thing in the morning. Its habit was that when it moved, its

battery would fall out and it would

turn off. He didn't have it and wanted to stay silent forever, and

leave me...

After struggling a lot, I couldn't turn it on again, I threw it in a

corner and got up. School was

starting, each of them were lying in the corner of the orphanage. For

several years, I always tried to

get to school on time, even once, and not listen to the assistant's

first morning advice, but I could

never experience this feeling...

The difficulty of waking up first thing in the morning, the unclear

meaning of breakfast, the parade

of irregular thoughts in my mind was my morning schedule

sometimes every day.

But in another way, it was better for me, because I had chosen the
pit when choosing between the
pit and the well, and that's why I took refuge in the school, where
there was no passion and only to
calm my ears, which was the advice of the family. He was tired, I
went to his school and classes,
otherwise, if he was a little sweet to me outside of school, I would
never even bother to pick up the
phone to ring his alarm clock...
I found the hem of my socks from under the closet of the room and
the other one from under me
mother's sewing machine, which was the companion of her
loneliness and the sound of which was the
night lullaby of my childhood, that sewing machine was the most
complicated device that I have ever
seen in human power. and the complexity of the tools that were
used in it makes me happy.
And that's why he had special respect in our house
I put on my socks and picked up my tired bag. I looked at my
weekly schedule so I wouldn't leave a book.
The only thing I learned from that lesson was by being forced to sit
in class...
Now the possibilities have their place.
I left the house with a frown, the weather was cold and dry
I was walking slowly without paying attention to the road...

My attention was caught between two constraints: the constraint of
life and the constraint of learning.
I had taken a narrow path between these two without settling and
staying in one of them...
Both of those constraints were like two artificial wings attached to
me by those around me to fly,
but they took me more to the valley than to the sky...
They were like two rollers on either side of me, spinning around me
and slowly squeezing me tighter.
I had lost control of my thoughts and today I hated school more
than ever.
I reached the side of the street and waited for a taxi until the old
arrow that was taking its last
breath like my phone stopped next to me:
Please sit in the back seat. The front seat needs to be repaired.
Yes, Sure
I sat in the back seat next to an old man
I looked out of the window and listened to the conversations
between the taxi driver and the old man
inside the car.
The old man's enthusiastic voice made me turn my head to look at
him
I saw
who is holding a sack of rice in his arms, he probably put his work
tools in it, it could be understood?
from his clothes that were sticking out from the corner of the sack

The old man had a warm conversation with the driver, he spoke so energetically and loudly that all
the cold, sleep and possibilities jumped out of my mind...
His words were so simple and sober that I could understand that there was no thought behind those words.
His words reached a point in the middle of the way
He pointed towards me and said to me:
For example, this young man now has to study for years to get a piece of paper as a certificate and look for a job.
How long should he go to school? How hard should he work?
In the end, like my son, he gets his bachelor's degree and sleeps at home, and his poor father has to
go to work every day like me to make ends meet.
Are there jobs for our youth now? The poor people are studying to become unemployed and stay at home.
Servant of God, his heart was burning for me and people like me and he said that they are not to
blame, there is too little work and everyone takes his acquaintance to work...
The driver, whose ears were full of these words, did not pay any attention to his words, nor did he pay
any attention to our present and future.
What was the benefit for him at all!?
He turns his head to find a traveler from the corner of the alleys so that he can turn his life around.

And in the middle of his words, he kept repeating that my chair has been broken for 3 days now and I
don't have money to fix it.
The words of that old man, at the same time, involved my mind and made me think...
I was in such an unfavorable mental and physical condition that I had no motivation or feeling to
continue and I was stuck like a piece of paper in the middle of the wind, and the wind of the fall of life
took me wherever it could, and wherever it wanted me. you beat
Sometimes with the discomfort of those around me
Sometimes thinking about the future
And sometimes by getting lost in everyday issues.
I always carried a feeling in my mind and heart that I did not know the origin of because none of the
people around me had smelled it.
And that was that the sadness of anyone I saw would change my mood in a few moments and anger
and sadness would take over my whole being.
And he kept me thinking about himself
And on the contrary, it was also true for me that their happiness also made me happy and gave me joy.
I couldn't pass anyone I saw indifferently, if I couldn't do anything, I would resent and feel sad for
the people who were in my way for days.

I was like a blank notebook where anyone could write their words and leave.
In the same taxi I was in, with that frowning, sleepless, and impatient state, I was sad for that old
man, and his unemployed son, even though my condition was not better than him, but in my dream, I
was planning for their lives to save them. 10th, for his hands, I thought that his companion of many
years was tired, he was also throwing back his clothes and it was torn...
Or for his blind eyes that could not see any hope in it.
And his forehead, which had gone through so many twists and turns of life, that now it was like awinding maze.
I was drowning in these thoughts for most of the days and hours, and in the end, I got nothing but
irregular heartbeats and a desire for pure solitude and depression.
I wanted to hug him and work for him, give him my money, maybe I can ease his sorrows a little.
Maybe those deep lines on his forehead that were the result of not laughing for several years will
fade and maybe his kind look will give me life.
With these confused thoughts and dreams, I reached my destination...
The bitter taste of unemployment after studying for several years and the sweet dream of seeing
that old man's smile became my breakfast that day.

After I got out of the car
The old man waved his hand to me out of kindness and simplicity,
and the taxi driver did not return
the rest of my money on the pretext of not having change.
I didn't care as much as with him
Let's talk about money
To be honest, I didn't feel like doing it.
I reached the school and was slowly going to the queue for our class,
when the deputy of the school
pointed at me with his hand and told me not to enter the queue, and
I realized that I was late to
school again and I should be punished.
I went back to the school door
All the children were neatly standing in line and a handful of them
were gathered next to the school
door, the same former people who always arrived late to school, I
also joined them.
We put ourselves in the crosshairs of the vice principal's
punishments and his words of advice.
After the end of the morning lecture, which was about competing
with neighboring schools and
increasing the honors of the school, the children who were in line
went to class, and we also went to
class after all the words and punishments that the deputy gave us.
We went to our class

I found an old chair in the corner of the classroom and sat down so as not to be in front of the teacher.

And we were waiting for our teacher of religions studies to arrive

I was staring at my feet, reviewing the events of that day in my mind, my body was sitting in a chair,

but my soul was floating in the midst of other people's lives and was sad and happy at the same fine.

All of a sudden, the whole class became silent and they stood up. I realized that the teacher had

entered the class and I forced myself out of the chair to stand up.

I wasn't used to showing respect to someone I didn't like, and he also understood this from the way I

got up and gave me a glance and put his bag full of books on the table and sat down.

As per his usual habit, he nodded his head up and down with a frown, which means please take your seat.

He stood up after attending to us

He looked at the weekly homework of some of the children and asked them a few questions, and then

started lecturing on monotheism and prophethood.

I wanted to ask him all the questions that were passing through my mind at that moment

Who else could give order to my tangled mind?

He was our moral teacher

But

In his class, when I wanted to ask a question

If I asked, my body and soul were so stressed that my heart began to race strongly and I regretted
asking the question... I couldn't say even one of them. Thank you, what about raising the questions
that were stuck in my confused mind, he said all the words he had prepared and packed his things and
left, and we stayed and a world of homework for the next week was on our shoulders. The task that
we carried on our shoulders for weeks and weeks and maybe years, and I never took them seriously,
and God never left me in his hands during the inspection of exercises and questions.
The class is over and We went to the school yard for a few minutes to rest
I could totally feel that I was in the presence of a different person from the others who was lost in
his thoughts and dreams
The enthusiasm and discipline of the rest of the students
Their ironed clothes and well-shaped hair meant nothing to me
To be honest, those things never mattered to me. Hunger made me go to the cafeteria of the school
and buy something to eat to get rid of the bitter taste in my mouth. We were standing in line for the
shopkeeper to let us in. In the blink of an eye, the children would snatch it from him and divide it in a
corner and eat it.

Groups of children were gathered in the school yard and each group had its own morals and fashion...
Some of them were talking about their exams and private classes, some of the elite competitions and
inventors who had registered, and the group to which I belonged were those children who were
always at the front of the yard because they were late. They were punished and a handful of people
gathered together and talked
And the topic of our discussions were funny words and jokes.
Sometimes we would all get together and begrudge the situation of one of us who was more miserable,
and the sadness would take over our entire being.
We never talked about the school and its classes; we all shared this point that we knew that the
path we are on does not give us any enthusiasm.
Our second class was the literature class, this made me happy and I attended the literature class
with enthusiasm, perhaps the only class in which I always attended with motivation and excitement
was the literature class.
Maybe this happened because of his good and humorous teacher
A teacher who was friends with 90% of the children whom the school did not accept as students at all
and who always caused trouble in the school, and because of this, he always spoke at the school, and

he was probably warned several times that he would be rude to the students. And keep his boundaries, especially those people who were not good for the school...

No position

Not high marks

And not discipline.

But that teacher always liked us and always filled us with love, kindness and hope in different ways

As if he knew that he should not leave us alone.

It's as if you understand all our inner sorrows from our faces

He was such a master in the literature lesson that he didn't take anything seriously...

And jokingly, he could teach us the whole book without us getting tired of that class for a minute.

We were so comfortable in his class that we could say whatever was on our minds

One time in the middle of his teaching, we came to a sentence from the book when we were checking

the word "Lal Lab*" in a poem, which is an adjective and which is a noun, etc.

One of the children jokingly asked the teacher, "Does the teacher have lips?"

And our literature teacher was a master of answering this type of questions, he looked with a little

---

A Persian term that compares the lips to jewels*

pause and laughed and mischievously said, "You don't have the tradition to understand this, your
father understands this better, ask him to tell you if he has lips or not!"
The whole class burst out laughing for a moment, we all laughed
The sound of our laughter was so loud that it didn't take long for the school principal to find us and
reminded us that the next class had an exam and asked for the class to be under control, and gave a
heavy look to our teacher and left...
Maybe he said in his heart that there are other breaths in the afterlife, soon we will expel you from
school so that we can take a breath.
By expelling him, maybe all our laughter and enthusiasm would be gone from school...
And many children may never even set foot in school
But fortunately, this did not happen while we were there
All the hours I was in school, I didn't know the meaning of time, only when we were studying literature,
I really forgot all the thoughts and worries that hit me every day, and it was as if that hour was the
hour of life for me, full of laughter and joy. Full life of literature lessons...
From his poems to the meaning of his words, from the biography of writers and poets to the sweet
story of Lili and Majnoon.

Especially when our literature teacher spoke in a pleasant tone.
When the class was over, I didn't go out for recess and we were
discussing a topic with one of the kids
until I came to my senses and saw that the next lesson was algebra
and probability, and this made
me a little excited and enthusiastic, but I still had it in my mind. I
was walking through the poems
and stories of the literature class
Little by little, the children returned to the classroom and prepared
the board to write the problems
and questions of algebra and probability
A boring lesson that at the end of the class squeezes our lives in the
midst of its complicated
problems
But as much as the lesson was boring and his teacher was a very
calm and patient person who never
got tired or maybe his fatigue reached the border of numbness.
In that class, we used to solve problems that our blackboard could
not fit the answer to and the
teacher always had to erase half of the board to fit the rest of the
answer.
This lesson, despite all its difficulty and the good teacher it had, had
no attraction for me, and I could
feel that the answers to the questions in my mind were never found
in the answers on the board, and

I was always forced to spend hours at home solving the exercises to pass the lesson I used to spend
time and in the end, I passed with a grade between passing and failing, which was also very acceptable for me.
Sometimes I felt sorry for his teacher and as always, I understood his annoyance and a tired face
that had solved many problems in himself for years.
Maybe he had many unresolved issues and we didn't know about it
After enduring the minutes and calamity of sitting in the class...
It was time to go home, half of the class woke up with the sound of the school bell and flew out of the
classroom door like birds trapped in a cage...
I was always the last person to leave the class, not because I wanted to stay in the class, but
because I didn't have that much enthusiasm to go out. I was sitting in my seat and my eyes were
staring at the blackboard and those answers the vague words that were printed on it with that old
man, and his unemployed son had created a painful combination in my mind... Among all the lines on the
board, I saw myself at the end of it, that I was finished and sitting at home without work.
I came to myself, the bitter silence of the class was covered by all the noise, I gathered my things,

got up and pulled my legs behind me to go out. When I left the class, I paused a little by the blackboard, I wanted to answer all those issues and questions. Draw a line and empty all the worries and thoughts that were holding me there and relax.
I removed the old chalk from the bottom of the board and found a small, untouched space in the
corner of the blackboard, and at that moment, my hands brought the words that were passing
through my mind to the board.
It is as if your heart is caught in the middle of a strong hatred
And no one knows about it
The fate of life and the fate of continuing in a tasteless path put pressure on my heart
This is how I celebrate the birthday of my first white poem in that heavy silence of the class...
One day I will release my whole body and soul from this swamp. Thinking of a beautiful beach, I head to the sea.
I wrote this sentence and muttered it to myself several times, every time I read it, I felt a sense of
liberation, as if someone from the outside took the clue of my pains and sorrows and killed it, as if he
was free from all my thoughts and mind. and fly in the blue sky of my heart.
I felt that something was created from me
which has music and rhythm and wants to convey a concept

And every time I read it, my soul and heart become polished and shine.

Now, like a thoughtless and happy boy, I was coming down the stairs, I reached the school yard, the snowflakes had drawn a white curtain on the yard, I was looking and I wanted to write the sentences that were passing through my heart on that whiteness of the ground, as if every heartbeat was a seed. He was publishing about love, and his bud was the sentences he gave to my mind, but I couldn't collect all of them in one place, so I bent down and drew some aimless lines on the snow with me finger and left...

I saw the children's footprints that were slowly disappearing among the snowflakes.

All that noise and bustle

All that talking and planning

All those threats and worries

Now they all gave way to the whiteness of the snow without any stains, and only I could see it because no one but me was there.

I came out of the school yard and entered the path from where I always return home. I walked slowly and with measured steps towards the taxi station. They were catching in the air. When I looked at them, I enjoyed their real excitement and joy, without realizing it, a smile would appear on my face...

One of those children had clenched his fist and was saying to his friends with stress, "I held the snowflake in my hand, now you are in trouble." There was nothing in his hand except a wet part that didn't last for a few seconds...

They were stunned and again, to prove that they can hold the snow in their hands, they jumped in the air and laughed...

Their world was sweeter and happier, just like my childhood, when I played for hours on the soil around our house, the smell of which still spreads in my soul, and every moment was new and exciting for me. I was in those moments when I was completely present. I had and I was enjoying what I was... I would make a path in the dirt and move a mud car through that path and take it to its destination. I would travel this path many times without getting tired...

And at the end, with my hands full of soil, I used to pile up a heap of dirt at the end of the path, and it was like a leafy mountain for my children, and I was proud of it...

The more I had distanced myself from my mindless childhood, the more I had trapped myself between the self-made chains of my mind and the margins of life.

Now I was so far away from those times and its joys that nothing makes me happy, or rather, I could be happy with less happenings.

Unless I saw happiness in the faces and happiness of the people around me and for a moment my heart would feel better
I was divided that day between the morning sadness of the old man and the joy of the children immersed in the game.
During half a day, mood swings and endless sadness and happiness formed in me
I was walking and my eyes were wandering around me. There was a feeling of happiness and vitality
outside. People were free and everyone was doing their work. Their lips were smiling and their faces were full of real joy and excitement.
The light snow gently fell on the ground, which was spectacular
I used to be happy when I saw them, I was ecstatic and enjoyed...
Every now and then, I saw young couples under the black umbrellas, holding hands, leaving traces of their romance on the white snow...
Indeed, there was nothing more enjoyable than that moment for them.
It's like if your whole world is one person and he is always happy by your side, what else do you want...
Don't pay attention to anyone else except that one person and let all your joys and happiness be shared...
What a sweet fence...
I didn't know from where, but at that moment, I was a combination of romantic and childish feelings,
happiness and excitement
I was standing in the middle of the sidewalk

A beautiful girl with smiling lips, as if she had never tasted sadness,
passed by me with her mother
wearing a hat and a white shawl that made her look more beautiful.
I could even smell the artificial flowers that were arranged for
decoration inside the shop.
My eyes fell on this girl, after she was a few steps away from me, she
quickly turned back and looked
at me, and I looked at her. I couldn't catch the scene...
I was only thinking that why is she looking at me and smiling, maybe
she understands what's going on
inside me and maybe she was attracted to the frowns that I carried
on my forehead, he didn't know
what a frown and sadness taste like.
A strange contradiction was formed between us
A little girl with a smile and full of enthusiasm and me who was full
of frowns and troubled thoughts
And maybe I was different among the people she had seen
I didn't have any other feelings, but this incident was different and I
kept wondering, especially what
makes me think the most is their girls' world, how tender and full of
kindness and love it was...
How carefully she paid attention to the details of her clothes and
how calmly and confidently she
walked, as if he was flying.
I was jealous of her for a few moments, I wanted to be in her place
and always have a smile on me

face and always spend my days happily...
But this was a dream for me...
I was far away from that time...
It was as if I had tied up that smiling, happy and full of emotion child...
And I had caught myself in a mire of thoughts and sorrows and everyday life.
I was talking to myself to organize my thoughts
Air boy enjoy it so well
The snow is so beautiful
Why do you always think of others?
Be happy, smile and thank God
I consoled myself the same way as I do always
I calmed down a bit and reached the crossroads
People were busy shopping and the market was crowded. There were few days left to Eid and many
people were seen on the sidewalks, markets and shops
The shopkeepers were shouting to sell their goods...
The goldfish that the little children put in the big pans...
And vegetables that decorated their waists with colored papers...
Everyone was promoting their goods and calling...
Yes, each person only the goods of his own shop.
But I was looking everywhere and I was looking everywhere as if I was looking for someone, and it felt
good to be among people, those crowds, those voices were exciting for me, I was a mixture of all the

smiles that were in the looks and faces of people. ...
And also, a mixture of those people who have not seen a smile on their faces for years.
From the feverish hands and face of the old man to the insensitivity of the taxi drivers...and the
working children who are always looking for something next in the trash cans unaware of them
surroundings. To make their day turn into night.
Half of my being was living in happiness; the other half was trapped in the deepest layer of sadness...
The buying and selling market were so hot that I wanted to shout something out loud and sell it or
talk to people to promote it, but I had no goods to sell, no one who wanted to talk to me, everyone was
busy with their own life, but I was not busy with anything. At all, I had no unfinished business to
pursue, so many people were rushing this back and forth that I envied them, I felt that I had lost me
way, or that the path I was on was not right, or maybe it was the other way around!! If I would talk
to them, they would envy me for being unemployed and carefree, and they were tired of the busyness of life.
The snow had become heavier, and I was waiting for a taxi at the crossroads
What can I say!! I was in no hurry to leave, and I wasn't looking for a taxi, I was standing alone and

my eyes were looking here and there.
A few steps away, someone caught my eye. In the midst of all the crowd, I saw an old man standing
next to a shop with his head down. I was curious to know what he was looking at with so much focus. I
saw him, but there was nothing under his feet, he was only holding a half-crumpled black bag in his
hand, he slowly moved in an unknown direction, even without paying attention to his surroundings, he
was going to the other side of the street, shrugging his shoulders from the cold. he was looking under
his feet and walking, sometimes bumping into people and passing by as if he didn't notice anyone.
I was following all the details of that man without any reason for doing so, it was different for me, I
was always looking for different people, my sense of curiosity always flowered about unusual issues, and I followed him.
The old man was in no rush or worry and no direction to go in the middle of all the crowd. I followed him as if he was familiar to me.
He slowly made his way to this side of the street and stopped a few steps away from a fish shop and
remained still again. After a few minutes, he moved out of the basket outside the shop, which was full
of fish lying on ice. He picked one and put it in the bag without looking inside the shop and even if

anyone noticed, he was walking away. He was holding her hand. He had not gone a few steps from the shop when the fishmonger came out of the shop and followed this man. He was wearing white boots and an apron with the blood of thousands of dead fish on it, grumbling under his breath and running behind the man. He moved greedily and the closer he got, the louder he shouted

Mr. Hoovi, you are stealing my fish....

O people, catch that old man...

That man is not one of the people around here, it is not known where he came from...

Catch that thief...

You steal fish from my shop in broad daylight.

You have to be a good old man...

I looked at the old man whose legs were weak, his hands were shaking and he was taking his steps forcefully, but he didn't pay attention to what was behind him, as if he didn't hear a sound at all and didn't notice anyone. He was holding the bag tightly in his hands and was moving. I couldn't see his eyes. I wanted to look at him and see where his eyes were looking...

All his movements were different from the people around him, he considered himself a stranger...

The feeling of escaping and staying had taken over his entire being

The dead fishmonger made his way through the crowd to the old man and put grabbed on the old man's neck from behind and pulled his shirt. If he wants to steal from my shop, you see, he is not ashamed at this age and he steals... The people were looking at the old man with eyes full of anger and one of them was saying that people like these have ruined the society.
One of the people was saying from behind the people, punish him, he is not from our area at all, obviously, he came here from somewhere else to steal... I opened my eyes and my heart rate had increased without realizing it, and anger took over my entire being, anger, excitement, curiosity, and even a sense of compassion. Without knowing the reason, there was a commotion inside me. I wanted to do something. I wanted to fight with that fish seller and pay for the fish. I wanted to stand up and fight against all the people who were angry, hating and taunting the old man? I had no weapon in my hand. Except for my heart beats which were getting more and more every moment
People who were lonely and oppressed were always important to me and I wanted to do whatever I could for them, I felt compassion, and this feeling was so great at that moment that anger and stress also overwhelmed me...

I was thinking in my heart, how much is a month worth to blame and argue with an old man like this...
In anger, he pulled the fish from the old man's hand and threw the black bag on the ground, and the blackness of the bag was more visible against the white of the snow, and he said that it is not clear what things he stole from this bag and who he made miserable. There is no side of us and he would go back to his shop with pride and running astray, while during this time, if someone had taken dozens of fish from his shop, he would not have noticed at all, maybe the same thing happened.
He left and the old man was left alone among the people and was looking at the bag that fell on the ground as if he wanted to pick it up, but the fast steps of the passers-by stole the bag from his sight.
They were judging him, he was passing by, he was walking calmly, as if his existence had been taken away from him, during this time, not a single word came out of his mouth and he did not look at anyone...
He was unable to walk, so I wanted to buy some of those fish for him and give them to him in private and apologize to all the people who broke him with their words and looks.

Tell him that whenever you need something, come to the shop, I will provide it for you. Maybe he needed these words, maybe if someone had intervened at that moment and not let the fishmonger make him feel this way, he would have hugged him and cried, maybe he was looking for a hand. To hold his hands, but no one paid any attention to him, except for the feeling of hatred and sarcasm and running astray from many people who made him feel heavy. But I had no language for these words and no money to buy fish. Only in my heart was full of chaos, I moved myself to go forward, my legs were dry with cold and stress, but a burning fire was burning inside me. I dropped it and my eyes followed his steps and followed him.
After he went away a little, he turned into an alley and got away from my eyes, maybe because he wanted to get away from himself with this amount of humiliation and eyes full of pity and bad mouth.
Maybe he can distance himself a little from the eyes full of anger and hatred
And maybe he is afraid that someone will come from behind him and take away the solitude that he now had the feeling of absolute loneliness...
At that moment, there was no more beautiful snow, no laughter, and no sound of any shopkeeper...
All my feeling of happiness subsided for a moment...
I felt all those shopkeepers

Their genders were fake...
Their screams were nothing but empty air and there was no emotion behind those voices...
I saw their hearts full of anger and hatred...
With this feeling of hatred, anger and sadness, we watched the alley
I forced myself to follow the old man and turned into the alley. He was walking a few steps away from me. I was looking at him.
Now he raised his head and didn't look at his feet anymore, as if a mountain had been lifted from his
back, he was slowly counting his steps. To take the moments and take all the words that were said to
him, maybe I could solve a little of his sorrows, and I would also remove the feeling of anger, hatred,
and compassion from my body and soul.
But when I came, I saw how uncomfortable these words from a 19-year-old boy are for an old man, and
he doesn't pay attention to my words, maybe he will tell me what you have to do with this...
And you, boy, don't need to console me...
Or maybe he will pass me by like all the people who passed by him without paying attention...
But I could feel his sorrows inside me, a person who was a stranger to the rest of himself
Even now, he was branded a thief
But he was not a thief...
He was never a thief.

Maybe he needed that fish, maybe he took it for his children
Maybe he had nothing to eat.
Maybe, like the old man in the taxi, he had a son at home who paid for his expenses...
He is a father; he doesn't want his children suffer anymore and that's why he did this...
I was in these thoughts when I saw an old man standing a few steps away from me with his back to me
I stood in my place like a nail, I didn't know what I wanted to say.
My train of thought was out of my hand, I didn't know what I wanted to say, but I felt that he
understood that I was walking behind him, my heart rate was fast...
It was as if my whole body and soul had been captured by emotion and kindness. I wanted to offer all
that love, kindness and intimacy to that old man.
He turned towards me, but his head was no longer down, he looked at me and a smile was on his lips.
As if he knew that I was walking behind him
I didn't see any sign of defeat, sadness or embarrassment in his face
I stole my eyes from him so I wouldn't look at him. I was ashamed.
I wanted to tell him that I want to buy you a fish.
But this was definitely not a joke for him.
He had green eyes and fair skin... I could feel the redness of my cheeks on my face, it was as if I stole something and he saw me...
He was looking at me and I had become a person at that moment, as if I was not the same person

that my heart was burning for that old man a few moments ago.
I was completely embarrassed
As if he wanted to help me, I had nothing to say, only our eyes were talking to each other and a smile
that was full of vague calmness and endless silence...
I was drowning in myself...
He was like a mirror and my image appeared in him; I saw myself in that mirror...
All the days that I had spent passed one by one in front of my eyes...
All those moments I had spent alone and no one had understood a bit of my inner feelings.
It was as if his eyes were looking at my whole past and I had become an actor at that moment when
he was watching my performance and there was a smile of satisfaction on his lips...
And I felt all the events and people that I was sad for years inside me, I came to my senses and
saw that the old man had moved away from me.
I had no other way to go and I didn't want to even take a step towards it, as if you are a small fish
and in the blink of an eye you will be thrown from a small strait to a big river.
I was dumbfounded and motionless. I was staring at the past and future events and the path I am in.
He looked at me and I saw myself.
I was alone for a few minutes and I was thinking about myself...

I was saying to myself; has he seen me and understood the things that I have thought!?

I didn't know, I really didn't know what was happening to me, but I was freed from all my thoughts and worries.

I had forgotten the whole story of that old man, except the look full of words and full of peace he had...

As if he understood that I want to help him take the burden of sadness off his shoulders and kiss his empty and cold hands...

Because he treated me as if I had done all those things for him and now, he has a deep sense of satisfaction on his face.

The words "thief" and "fishmonger" and the anger that was in my eyes all left my body and soul...

I was like a piece of wood floating on the surface of the sea without any thoughts or worries...

I could feel my feet walking slowly on the ground and they were enjoying. I followed my gaze, people, objects and everything became beautiful in my eyes again.

Everything I saw around me was as if it was the first time when I passed by them again and again every day.

And I had never seen them like this, everything felt new to me, I felt that I had won the game in which I had played for years.

Like a child who wants to let his father know that he is a hero, and I had become a hero at that moment, and a great sense of power spread throughout my eyes and soul...

I chased him with my eyes until he disappeared from sight and left...

My heart found its regular beats
That old man left and I stayed and a world of silence full of words, full of experience full of unspeakable things that were more expressive...
And I was filled with the song of silence that plays me in the best way every moment...
He was familiar to me; I saw that man in the depths of my being and I was close to him...
As if he was me...
Days passed and I was abandoned in the flow of life...
Every day I realized more about my differences with the rest of society, but this incident did not
make me avoid people. I was a mixture of people. My whole body, soul, and all my feelings needed people.
But what separated me from them was a part of my soul that lived in each person
He was happy with their happiness and sad with their sadness
I was not one person, I was a combination of different people's lives
For example, there were days when watching a movie about a baby deer being eaten by a lion, I would
feel compassion for hours, and for several days I would put myself in her mother's place and feel the
pain she was going through, maybe even more than her mother herself.
Now, for the inconvenience of humans, which is much more...

In contrast to those sorrows, everyone's happiness also made me
happy and revived the buds of happiness and hope inside me...
At night, I got home with these thoughts and experiences that I had,
I put blue on my face and looked
at myself in the mirror. I was different from the previous days, how
much my face had become hot and
how vaguely painted I had become. I looked
You could understand that my face was sadder than it could bear,
and maybe the only person who was
not sad was myself...
I sat at the table again, oblivious to myself, who had disappeared.
What are we having for dinner, mother?
Dill rice with fish
Half of a healthy fish, whose head was not even removed from its
body. When I looked at the fish, me
mind drew me to the past of the fish and to those who were waiting
for that fish, who may have been
waiting for him in a pond.
I took hold of my thoughts again and:
Son, this is human food and everyday thousands of fish are caught
and eaten by humans, but now
many fish are eaten by sharks and...
I had read somewhere in the books that it mentioned the laws of the
forest that many animals must
become food for other animals, otherwise the cycle of the forest and
nature will not be complete...

The essence of those laws was to eat until you are eaten, or the animal that is stronger will survive...
Indeed, this issue also applies to the cycle of human nature? But humans don't eat each other
why
Maybe it applies to humans in different ways and different from animals
You should never be eaten
Or someone will destroy you directly!!
Sometimes the beat of your kindness makes you feel slower and slower
Rather, the greatness that is inside each one of us and originates from a great power in the name of
God is eaten in different forms of the soul and existence of humans.
For example, those who have more power have a better life than the weak and the poor, and they use
them to maintain their comfort and have better food than them, or many other issues are different...
Thoughts came to my mind from all directions, they were like spools of cotton, each of which had its
own color and smell, and each of them rushed to my mind to weave something, but the thread of me
thoughts were not in my hands; I did not know what should be woven.
In an unconscious current, all I had to do was to flow

I pulled the last tiny fish bone out of my mouth and felt the
delicious taste of fish in my soul
I turned off all the voices in my head and told myself that I should
live the other side of the story as
well, that I shouldn't mourn for anything, so every day I get older
and more depressed than yesterday.
From now on, I will enjoy everything and put myself first in
everything
All that exists is for my comfort and I must use it
I will not suffer anyone's sorrow anymore and I will not do anything
for the happiness of others,
except what they have done for me except that they have left me
alone in deep sadness.
I hate myself with greed and anger and I was planning for myself
+ After I finish my military service, I come back, I buy a hook and
catch fish, and I pull them out of
the water alive and watch them die, and then I fry them in the
middle of a burning fire and eat them.
I go to the rivers, I enjoy and have fun, and my mind calms down a
bit
But also get rid of compassionate thoughts for all beings.
Although I hated this decision, I said these things to myself and put
my head on the pillow and slept
The days passed by quickly
After waking up in the morning to go to school and repeating daily
routine and monotonous life,

I found myself on top of a hill where my teeth were grinding each other from the cold and I had to
keep my legs straight....
I had a rifle in my hands, the weight of which made my shoulders dry and hurt, I was wearing a dirty
dress with boots that were polished every day...
For an hour I was standing on that high and soulless hill, and I was staring at the border that was
marked for us and we should be watching and paying attention to it all day long....
I took out an old notebook from my pocket and ticked the end of the ninth month of enlistment and
put it back in my pocket and continued waiting for the next month to arrive...
For a few moments, I witnessed my thoughts passing through my mind at the top of that hill...
I am happy that it is not my turn to eat dinner today...
Or in two days, it will be my turn to take a bath until all my poetic and romantic feelings disappear.
Just as I decided to get rid of compassionate and kind thoughts a few years ago, now the times had
gotten rid of me and put me in the crosshairs of unkindness, indifference, and hardships.
The joy of those days was my hair, which had grown a little longer and now I could give it direction....

Or in a few days I will get my leave card and I will sleep at home without stress or worry even
without knowing what the border is.
And my shoulders felt numb from the fatigue of the gun...
What a rare thing had happened to me, from my worries to make others happy and my happiness near
Eid and the mood of shopping and sightseeing. Now I was standing in a place where not even a car had
passed by for months. I longed to see people. have been.
I was told since I was a child that being a soldier makes a man out of a boy and makes him strong!!!
The worries of my past years, which deeply upset me, the desires of my every moment, I had become
further and further away from people, and a strange feeling had taken over my whole being.
At night, with complete exhaustion, I reached the wall of the dormitory and sat on the stone that
accompanied the cries and heartache of the former soldiers.
I put my back on the ground and placed its tube under my chin, leaned on it with my hands and kept
my eyes fixed on the light that was on from the other side of the border in the neighboring country.
A few steps away from me, a servant whose name was Ali was polishing his boots, the sound of the
polishing brush rubbing against the boots felt exactly like sharp glass rubbing against the veins of my heart.

which killed the roots of the feeling of love and affection in me.
I called Ali
I said, Ali, what are you doing? What are you thinking, don't you miss anything?
Are your days going well or not?
He didn't understand anything from my questions, he just told me that days are going by.
I said, Ali what wish that will make you happy if it happens?
He said that my wish is to finish my service and go to our city to help my father reach us
agricultural and livestock lands.
What do you wish for? You are always yourself, what do you think about?
I said, do you know what my wish is, Ali?
He said maybe you want to go on vacation for ten days, right?
I said no
Ali, I miss seeing people, I don't know how to tell you, but I really miss the unkindness, the lack of
understanding,
I want people to be around us now and I can grieve among them like before, but I want them to be me
existence depends on their sadness and happiness, without them there is no passion and intelligence in me.
Ali was in an unknown silence, I don't know if he understood me or not, but he didn't say anything and
didn't show any reaction to my words.

That was enough for me

I continued to tell him that I have another wish, and that is that in the history of human life, there

should be an hour in which all the people on the planet will be happy and happy, and everyone who

tries to make others happy will always fulfill this wish. I have it with me

I am sure that at a certain time of the year, all people are happy and full of kindness.

Ali gave me a satisfied smile and took my hands and lifted them up and said it's time to sleep, we

should rest for the next post.

In my vague dream, we moved to the rest area and I lay down on my bed.

I put my head on the pillow and my eyes were fixed on the top of the bed. I was staring at the

writings that the soldiers had written on the bed and the wall of the barracks many years ago. I saw

a sentence that was written in bad handwriting under the upper bed. I cut it so that I can read it...

wrote:

As I write this, you are asleep...

And when you read this, I'm sweetly asleep.

I read this sentence, in order to understand it, I put myself in the place of the person who wrote this

several years ago, and I thought about him, and now that his military service was over and he was
asleep and I was reading this...
I couldn't sleep because of the things that happened to me, and even more than that, I had the
feeling of someone who has lost his way and is moving towards an unknown destination. My body and
soul seemed to not be mine.
That night, one of the children, who was bothered by shortness of breath and woke up several times
every night to get oxygen, got up and after his breathing calmed down a little, he saw me awake...
He came and sat next to me.
A kind and well-spoken boy whose literary structure was meaningless to him...
As always, I used to laugh when I saw him...
He said, "Dad, I'm laughing."
what happened Armin
I said with a smile, are you really upset?
He said I want to hurt you
I thought he would say funny and rude things like always.
But no! Armin was different that night.
It was as if everyone was different that night, each of them was sad and sad
He was telling me about his failed love.
I lost my life in this army,

Before I came here, I was a nurse in a big hospital where I saw
different and good people every day
and I was surrounded by girls that I fell in love with one of them....
I did everything for her, I took him wherever he wanted, and I
didn't miss anything for her. I loved her
so much that I bought her the most expensive wedding flower so
that she would stay by my side.
We had gone everywhere together, and I wanted to marry him, but
his father gave me a condition
that I must finish my military service so that he would agree to give
me his daughter. It wasn't a
week after my service that when we were allowed to call from the
dormitory, I called my love. She
didn't recognize me for a few seconds until I clearly explained
myself to her and he apologized to me
and said that I have a suitor.
I love her and I want to marry her.
I could taste that word and no one will understand that moment in
that military hardship until they
are caught in that situation themselves.
As he used to say, the anger took hold of my throat and made me
number than ever...
I said it means it's over...
He said that I could not say anything at that moment
I just said

I did so much for you, I bought anything you wanted, and I gave up
my work and life for you, I joined the
army, now you say that you want to get married....
So, what about all the deep emotional relationship between us?
Those sentences you always told me about endless love?
And he also said, well, I have my own life, you will be in the army
for two years, and after that, it is
not known what will happen, and I cannot throw my life back.
I still can't believe this happened and I have no motivation and hope
now that I am here....
I couldn't say anything to him, I thought a little bit about this
incident in this situation, it made me
sick, now you think that I would be in that situation
I forced my mouth open and told him that you are a great man...
And God always arranges these events for great people
If this happened to me, maybe I wouldn't be able to bear it.... I was
consoling him when he got up and
shook my hand and went to his bed and slept....
I could not sleep that night until the morning...
You know there, even thinking about another person's romance was
new and fun for me, the only thing
we had was thinking and thinking... and spending days in fantasy...
You think about what you want and you are happy with them...
what funny days
Day by day, we were getting bigger and rougher and our emotions
and feelings were fading...

The hardships of the cold and staying awake at night and the events
we saw had turned us into the
man, that society wanted
A rigid man who is no longer affected by small events...
He learns to skip many things easily...
And pass through emotions and feelings without stopping...
The only joy of those days was the saying that one day we will
remember the things we are going
through and we will laugh about them.
And I never laughed at those days in my life
After spending months, I finished the story of the soldier
The environment outside the barracks gives me a breath of fresh air
Like a fish that returns to the water after a while, everything that was
outside had the color of
freshness, vitality and enthusiasm for me.
When I got home
After all the ceremonies and the slaughter of the sheep whose
oppressed eyes are still haven't faded
in front of my eyes... I continued on the path of life again....
One day, I had decided to save myself from all this compassion and
kindness and troubled thoughts,
and going to the army helped me a lot in this decision.
To strengthen the sense of power of indifference inside me, I went
to a river around the city to fish.
I had learned to think only about the pleasure of catching and eating
fish, its taste and smell, and all

the sorrows of the fish and their families from my mind.
I prepared his equipment and turned towards the river and moved. I found a small flat land by the
river and I spread my net and sat down, and I was preparing my hook...
The river was a bit turbulent, and the fish were stitching their heads out of the water, diving into
the air, and diving back into the water. Certainly, the fish that lived in the water all their lives,
jumping into the air was new to them and it was very enjoyable, as Humans live their whole lives on
land, they find swimming in water much more enjoyable.
Does this story also apply to our beliefs and views??
For example, the beliefs that have remained untouched in our minds for several years and have been
passed on to us, and we are also passing them on untouched!?!
Do they also like to change and see another way of the world from time to time?
It was a question that passed through my mind like a chain
I sat by the grass around the river and looked at it. I picked up a stone and threw it towards the
river. I had seen this many time in romantic movies or romantic scenes of two lovers, where people
sit by the lake and throw stones into the sea. And they put a cigarette on their lips and create a

strange and romantic feeling in themselves, but I was only playing that role and I didn't have any
feelings from this scene, whether now or in the years to come....
Except for the end of that stone under the sea and how long it should stay there and where it will
end up, I would not get anything...
The heat of the sun prompted me to get out of these thoughts and prepare my hook.
I attached the paste that I had prepared in advance to the tip of the hook, and I didn't get anything
when I threw my hook, I didn't know how to do it, I just wanted to catch fish.
After trying several times, I felt the vibration of the hook handle
It was as if a small fish had hugged my hook with the intention of getting food for it and was trapped.
When I pulled the hook, my heart started beating when I saw the moment the fish died involuntarily,
and my hands immediately took the fish off the hook and threw it into the river. As the fish in the
water had come to a new life; my heart became calmer and calmer...
And my fishing story book was closed there and I never cast a hook in the river again...
I lied down there and closed my eyes and tried to calm my thoughts and enjoy where I am and the
sound of flowing water was the best lullaby I ever heard.

After a while, I woke up and sat down, unaware of myself and my surroundings
From a distance, I saw an old man who had his pants up to his knees and was coming towards me with
muddy feet and a sack on his back.
He came closer and sat next to me. He put his sack on the ground.
It was full of half-sized gourd
fishes, all of which had died.
He told me, young man, you could not catch anything.
The other side of the river has come up and is full of fish, you can go and fill your bag there....
I said no, I don't know, and I only came here to sit and enjoy the air, I didn't come here to catch fish.
I was thinking that at this age, I will live so comfortably and indifferently towards animals and the
environment around me. I was somehow envious of that old man...
Now think about how he will eat them...
He said to me, come and take some of these fish, it's too much for me, I come here every day and catch fish...
He spoke in a tone that he wouldn't care if I took all his fish, and he didn't raise an eyebrow.
So that they don't tell me at home how many hours you went fishing and you couldn't catch anything,
I took some of his fish and put them in a bag to take home.
I asked the old man; what do you do with all these fish you catch every day? Do you eat them all? He

said no, my son. I haven't eaten fish for several years. I take them to the market and sell them. My
grandfather left us an inheritance and wherever there are many customers
I sell
That old man was someone who had been selling fish for several years and he was so calm that you
could not find any noise in him, as if all the happenings around him could not worry or upset him, just
the opposite of me, where even a small movement of a spider could take over my mind. close and trap
me in a cocoon of thoughts...
In that old man, I could see the inner peace that he carried with him for years, this could be
understood from the fact that he did not pay attention to me and that he did not ask me any other
questions...
At that moment, it came to my mind to fix and rent a small shop and in order not to have that old
man stand by the door in that cold and heat, I can do something and earn money.
I laughed and told the man my offer, even though it was going through my mind that he has been
selling fish on the side of the market for several years, so he should accept my offer, but with utter

surprise, the only thing he said was that it will get better, my son, and with He agreed with full satisfaction and said that if this happens, I will spend more and more time fishing and bring more fish to the shop. The truth is that selling fish takes more of my time and I get tired of talking to people. You are doing me a great favor I realized that he was satisfied with the minimum amount of money he could spend his day with while talking to me.
He should spend his income every day on the same day and that's it. A few days passed after that incident, and I rented a ten-meter shop and bought a second-hand refrigerator and kept it inside to keep the fish frozen. As the fish froze from the cold, I had become numb to them. And they had become normal for me Once every two days, the old man brings me fish with his basket and without saying a word or asking me for money, with a smile full of deep sadness and superficial calmness, he would throw the fish into the refrigerator and leave, and I would sell them too. It was going and my thoughts had become much better and better in the midst of buying and selling and communicating with people Every day I would sell almost all the fish that the man brought and I would put all the money in the

desk drawer and we would halve together. Day by day our sales would increase and increase, but this matter did not make any difference to the old man; it did not matter how much money he got or how much money We find out that it has been several years that he knows that he will receive what is in his mind from God that very night and leaves...
Without any expectations and without any objections...
He just didn't want to deal with anyone anymore
And for this issue, he was thanking me as if I had saved him from a big problem.
Does that mean it was so difficult for him to talk to people?
Or maybe they bothered him so much that he didn't even want to talk to them anymore??
He was running away from the market and his people...
But he was strangely fine by the river...
I was the opposite of him, the more I interacted with people during the day, the more passionate I felt
In particular, the distress of my thoughts became less and less
Several years have passed since this incident...
I was so stuck between buying and selling that I had turned my small shop into a store with daily efforts where we sold other things besides fish.
But still, all those fishes that the old man brings me were reserved and full of blessings for the store.

My work had taken a toll, my mood had changed so much that I no longer considered anything
important to me and I did not miss the pleasures of eating and sightseeing for myself.
I woke up in the middle of the afternoon, opened my closet and looked at my colorful clothes, and
among them I took the navy color which was also the color of the year and put it on, I combed my hair
and put a bitter cologne on myself with a sweet feeling and I was on my way out. I became
In the middle of the road, I visited the store, which was full of people, where three or four people
we're working and they were letting customers in, and everyone was satisfied with their work. They
brought me tea and sweets and seated me with special respect
My eyes were filled with power, fame and respect...
I had a strange feeling that my eyes could no longer see anyone but myself.
And my attention was not distracted anywhere except accumulating more wealth and experiencing new things
The time had come when my ten-meter shop had become a few-hundred-meter shop, and I would enter
it only to visit and receive a sense of pride and honor, and I would forcefully stay there for a few
minutes.

I had strengthened all the walls outside myself, but the wall of my heart had become thinner and
thinner, heartless and unloving.
Little by little, I wanted to get up and leave, my eyes fell on a man outside the shop who, in the crowd,
away from the eyes of the employees, took a fish from the basket and left. I reached that man
through the crowded crowd, my eyes were wide open with anger and he could not see anything around him
It's like all my possessions will be stolen
I reached that old man from behind, took the fish from his hand and pulled it, and in a harsh tone I
started cursing and returned.
Without my eyes noticing anyone except that fish, it was as if I had conquered a peak and I had also
taken the medal from that victory from the hands of that old man.
I threw the fish into the basket and told the children in a loud voice inside the store, "Where are you
paying attention? If it wasn't for me, they would have stolen the fish and I asked them that if they
don't pay attention, I will deal with them seriously... I said this from I left the shop...
I got into the car and drove around the city with pride and a special style that I had taken for myself
I was lost between the smell of cologne and the respect of the people around me and the pride that now took me

After all the secrets of not having a feeling of compassion and disturbing thoughts for others, I had
now become someone who sees people but himself as dim and the events around him were not important to him at all.
Now there was no news of those people whose sadness made me sad and whose smiles gave me life.
I had accepted even the weak animals are being eaten by other animals as a rule and I had
understood that in the game of life you have to go through many things easily in order to survive.
Where was the time taking me?
The only sense of power, fame, and wealth had become important to me...
Sometimes during the day, my controversial past and those thoughts that were always with me would
take over me and all those feelings would pass through my head...
But it was meaningless to me...
And I was lonelier than before
Now nothing was enjoyable for me anymore, I felt like I had tasted all the sweets in the world.
And all my days passed more pointlessly than before
I considered helping others inferior thing to do and during the day I was all focused on my clothes
and the pride I had made for myself...
It was my daily job to protect the honor and dignity that was attached to my legs like a bandage

The pride and prejudice that I had found were like spider webs that were woven around me and every
day they captured me more and more and made my heart beat slower and slower and most
importantly there were no traces of love, kindness and friendship in my heart. was not left
And that endlessly kind and compassionate heart of mine was now a piece that just beats without
releasing a particle of its nature, which was full of kindness and love.
Now there was a time when I had to force myself out of bed in the morning and even choosing clothes
and hairstyles and choosing the scent of cologne had become difficult and tiresome for me, and to
escape from these things I would sleep until late afternoon and I had been away from work, I had
considered myself to be the person who was respected among some people in the society, and this
greatness was like a widening trap that trapped me more and more in ego and loneliness.
This greatness and feeling of pride and ego happens for me and for humans when we are imprisoned in
weak and superficial beliefs like a prisoner.
And as time passed, life became harder and worse for me, and even when I talked to people around me, it bothered me…
One night, I received a text massage, when I opened the phone and read his name, he was one of me

old school friends and he invited me to celebrate his 38th birthday...
You could understand his enthusiasm from his message...
Why was he happy?
Because he was 38 years old?
Or to dance in the crowd?
And maybe his body was impatient for dancing, and this issue was not exciting for me from the
beginning, and I don't know why I hated congratulations, cakes, and birthdays. I considered these
things necessary for children because they are the roots of a They were mature people, the happier
and livelier they are at that time, their leaves will be more fertile and fuller of love in adulthood,
and they can be involved in spreading more love, kindness and happiness in the society, but if in
adulthood, for someone who has roots It has not seen enough water and suitable soil, no matter how
much you decorate its branches and leaves, it still hurts inside and deep, and this is undeniable.
I don't remember one time; the children had a birthday party for me and they had neatly placed me in
a stylish chair and they had prepared and decorated a cake and put candles in front of me. They
wanted to see the joy in me. which was rare for me for many years and this incident had a special
attraction for them

I played the role of surprised people for them and they had a lot of fun. They enthusiastically told me
to close my eyes and make a wish. No light from it entered my heart, and I did not inhale any pleasant
spring breeze into my lungs through it...
I could not accept that something would happen in my life years later to make me happy.
I had nothing but this moment, I could not imagine any future in front of my eyes...
I was not pursuing any goal
My forward movement was the only movement towards the past, the past and the past until I reach
my childhood and everything bring me joy and enthusiasm and I live my life as full as possible with
astonishment and vitality. Truly, childhood is the best period of life. It is human beings
A period when the traps of the mind and thoughts have not yet formed in you...
With all my efforts, I turned off the vague thoughts that were passing through my head and I heard
the voices of those around me saying, hurry up, boy, the candles have run out.
And repeating the same incident that I said at the end of the story that I made my wish and they
clapped for me and I blew out the candles and blew out all my thoughts with them...

Sometimes far from those beliefs and attitudes that were formed in me towards celebration and happiness
A good feeling filled with excitement like a thunderbolt filled me, but immediately a curtain of
sadness and sadness covered it...
I don't know where this happened, but I know that my beliefs of many years and my past full of
loneliness and stillness were involved in it.
A past where every little thing destroys me
And the passage of time had multiplied my loneliness
Over time, I deeply felt the lack of understanding between people
Finally, the night of celebration has arrived
And I was prepared for that birthday with well-groomed appearance and stylish clothes, as if
something wanted to happen to me and change me. I had fallen in love with changes that could
change me from the roots.
And it brought me back to the happy days full of feelings and kindness of the past
The birth was supposed to take place in a big garden that my friend's father had prepared for him
When we entered the party, everything was full of glitter and gold decor, in the middle of a big three
-tiered cake reception, and behind it was a chair full of decorated balloons and artificial flowers... a

few friends. I saw my school friends, which I hadn't heard of for a long time, after saying hello and
seeing the new faces and the changes that had been made in them, I sat down.
We were talking to them from a distance. I wasn't used to working in parties and gatherings like this.
I always sat in one place, and every now and then we joked with the kids and laughed...
For them to sting me
One of the kids was saying loudly how long do you want to be alone at parties
Find a companion for yourself.
The girls who were there and were busy arranging fruits and sweets heard this and looked at me and
said don't listen to them at all. Those who got married also regretted and couldn't be good companions
for each other...
From their words, I realized that some of the friends had also been married once and were finishing
it and were doing the final things of their divorce...
I was happy to be alone
At the very least, I was one divorce ahead of several children...
Many of the children in the group, many of whom were married and many others were single like me,
had come there and were decorating and picking cakes and food items.

The sense of satisfaction, euphoria and happiness could be completely felt in single ones
On the other hand, the neat clothes of the married people and the fact that they could not stop talking about their wives
The most enjoyable part of this birthday for me was the food that I ate to my heart's content, and after all the talk and laugh and the dance of the couples and the dance of the singles, I got tired very quickly and fell on the floor because of the excitement in it. I was enjoying the moment
I was experiencing an absolutely free feeling with an empty inside that had no romantic feelings or pride or any other vague feelings...
After a while, the children also got tired and sat down
And we got together little by little and one of the children suggested a game and with the majority of the children it was decided to play the dare and truth. I liked this game because I always asked questions that could not be asked to anyone in normal situations. I could ask them. This gave me a sense of curiosity and excitement. I could measure people's hearts with the questions I ask and know the depth of their experiences in life....
When the game started, I was the one who had to ask questions, and I chose someone to ask

questions who encouraged me to be single, and since for me the world of girls was very vague,
unattainable and unpredictable, there were always questions. I was asking that maybe in the opinion
of others there is no point in raising those questions and it will take the atmosphere away from
joking and laughing...
One of the special questions that I asked one of the friends was where will the end of this world go?
The girl looked at me and closed her eyes
He was exhausted, he had nothing to say, he forcefully said with a laugh, "Well, in the end, there's
nothing, what do you want to happen, we're going to die, it's over."
When he said this, they all laughed and I smiled too, and I couldn't expect anything but this answer
from him.
Maybe this simple and unhesitating answer that he gave is the answer to the whole mystery of us
world.
What does it want to be?
The end is nothing...
We die, it's over...
Is it really like that?!?
I do not know.
After thinking a little about this answer and the question that I have been thinking about for years,

I included this answer in my mind and told myself that this is the answer, the end is nothing....
After all the games and questions and laughter that were exchanged between us, my friend's
view of me changed a little and they kept the atmosphere heavy because of me because I was not
interested in silly jokes or unnecessary words and my jokes Most of the time, there were serious
words hidden in it...
The friends got tired and they all got up and left with the same excuse. I also went to the food and
ate some of each and came and sat down.
Some of the children went outside the yard to take pictures and some of them were preparing for
their own birthday party with their sweethearts, and they were describing to each other and having
a lot of fun.
Some people were talking to each other in the corners of the yard and house and talking about a
bright future together.
I started a conversation with one of the girls who was sitting on the other side and was not busy
with anything
I wanted her to tell me more about her girlish world and I asked her questions that were difficult for
her to answer. It is enough for us, and she laughed too...

After a few seconds, she said, of course, saving your presence.
She gave a short answer to my question, and I didn't ask any questions for a few moments...
I was thinking to myself, what does she mean? Aren't the boy's human, or when I looked at the depth
of the story, I said that maybe a serious damage has been done to the roots of her beliefs and has
brought her to this point of view.
A sarcastic sentence:
"Boys being human is enough for us."
She also asked me to ask a question
Be sure to ask whatever is on your mind...
She said why are you single? Why don't you get married??
She expected me to tell her that I am committed to a long-term love and that my eyes do not see
anyone except that one person, and now she is gone and left me alone, and I am in deep failure...
But I only said one word to her and that was "I don't know"...
And I really did not know why I am not married and why I am still single...
Instead of these issues occupying my mind, I occupied my mind with questions that were meaningless
in their opinion
What will happen to her last life...?
Why did humans get so far from each other?
Why has affection, purity, and intimacy become so much weaker?

And why have I moved away from my childhood...
The same crowd that was present there were a few lonely people who had gathered together without a bit of common ground, without a bit of fusion, each of them had their own world, even those couples who were there...?
There was no place left in my mind for a question like why I am not married...
But I knew that in order to get married, you must definitely prepare enthusiasm, motivation, and a predetermined goal for yourself in order to be in a position that I had never even thought about...
I realized that my answer did not feel good for her and he only said that I hope you will get married.
I felt that my answers were completely unexpected for her and She could not understand my words,
and She no longer had the desire to ask questions.
Instead of thanking her, I went back and asked her why you are not married...
She said, I won't bore you with my detailed story. I said that it was sweet for me to hear the words and the pain of the hearts since I was a child, even though in the last few years I have withdrawn myself from people and become more and more distant, but I will be happy if you tell me do

I asked her to say whatever She wanted because I could see that She was carrying a strange feeling
and a deep failure. You could understand this from her eyes full of chaos and sadness.
Especially after seeing her friends doing all kinds of romantic things to each other, she was
completely thinking and dreaming about him.
Maybe in her life he also liked to dance next to the person She loves and tell him about their future
together and pamper him.
Maybe not like this at all
She told me:
It was my last year of nursing when I went to one of the big hospitals in the city to finish my course...
I was so excited that I wanted to take off my wings
I was experiencing the same feeling that every girl wishes to experience. I had made my family proud.
I was happy and I saw a bright future in front of me. Our families would come to the hospital from
time to time to see me in a nurse's uniform...
And they were very happy
Some of my friends were also gathered there and we were experiencing the endless feeling of good
and happiness together....
From our secret jokes and laughs to getting to know a new environment and the excitement of giving

injecting and IV
As she was explaining to me, I was staring at a corner, and I was absorbing her words literally to me
bone marrow.
continued....
After we got home from work, we would go out together and go on nature trips, province tours, and
other girly pleasures.
Days passed and some of the boys who had just graduated joined us, and little by little, we started to
talk to each other. For some time, each of them was doing their own work and we had formed a group
of enthusiastic nurses there....
Little by little, our girlish talk increased and my friends talked more about the boys' work, praising
some of them and rejecting some of them.
At noon, they would tell me that Nima brought me tea today, and the rest of the children jokingly
told him that she liked you and that bringing tea is a sign of love, and we laughed.
Little by little, the atmosphere is girly and we had fun talking about boys and their jobs.
I was the only girl who didn't enter the privacy of boys, I wasn't so close to them that they offered
me something or wanted to help me... I was always a girl who was completely focused on her own work

and her girlish world.
Some of my friends had found boyfriends for themselves and they talked all day about their outings
or the gifts they gave each other.
I had slowly become more and more lonely and spent most of the day in my own world and tried to
focus more on my work and my passion for nursing...
My friends had also distanced themselves from me and spent most of their time with their love and
their boyfriends
One day, Bina, my friend was coming towards me with a smiling face and pointed to me with her hand
to come to the room... As soon as we entered the room, she closed the door and said to me on the
phone, Shida, do you know what happened? I said, something happened? Why are you panting so much?
She said that Nima says that one of his friends has been eyeing you since he came here and he liked
you and told someone to keep her, but Nima told me and I told you...
I smiled and said go get your card...
Leave this ridiculous game aside...
He said, I'm serious, Shida, one of Nima's friends is the same guy, who is a down-to-earth and very
unprofessional, his name is Ermine.

Without thinking about this, I said, "Don't bring me into your dirty game." I laughed and kicked out the door...

Mobina also told me from a distance, hopefully we will play together...

I turned back and gave her a sad look and went to visit the patients...

All the hospitalized people were doing well and they were thanking me more and I could feel their love and affection...

That night, when I got home tired and exhausted, I laid my head on the pillow...

I remembered Mobina's words...

And the thoughts that are spinning in my head, who is that boy who is watching me? Does he really like me?

Does that mean he loves me?

Why did he like me, why did he talk to me at all?

I tried to imagine the boy Mobina was talking about, but because I hadn't looked carefully and hadn't seen him, I couldn't figure out who he was...

I fell asleep with these questions in my mind...

The next day, while I was busy preparing one of the patients, I saw one of the children staring at me from a distance. I came into the room.

My hands were shaking uncontrollably and my heart started beating faster. I had never experienced any emotional connection with anyone until then...

For me, that moment was like a thunderbolt that hits the calm sea and causes chaos on the surface of the sea for a moment.

I tried to calm myself down. I knew that the boy was the same boy that Mobina said. I could accept what Mobina said at that moment. I took a deep breath and raised my head to go to the patient.

On the way, I glanced at him and saw someone there. was not I took a deep breath and calmly did my work....

In short, this story passed and until Armin and I spent half of our work day together and half of the rest of our work we were together outside...

He loved me so deeply that I enjoyed in the shadow of this love and spent days full of love and romance...

Armin was a quiet boy; would you believe me if I said that the only thing, he knew was to only think about me

I loved him too and it was as if life would not taste so sweet for me without him.

Days passed and Armin suggested that they would come to propose to me this weekend

He was in a hurry to do this and wanted us to get engaged as soon as possible, as if he was afraid

that we might not be able to get together, and he always told me that our lack of thought and
separation from each other drives him crazy.
Even though my mother agreed with this, my father always put this case on hold…
That ominous night, the marriage proposal arrived and Armin father, mother, sister and himself came
to our house, while all the people who were in our house were happy and cheerful, but Armin seemed to
be thinking about something or seemed to be drawing in his thoughts and was nerves.
This was not a good feeling for me at all, my eyes were on Armin and his unknown discomfort made me
stressed and worried
After talking about this, and beating around the bush, finally they started talk about marriage, and
at that moment, a strange feeling wandered in me, the feeling of always reaching the person with
whom I had all my romances, I had the feeling of flying in the middle of the sky, Ermine by my side. I
felt like forever
They were waiting for an answer from us
My father paused for a moment and said that we don't know much about your family and culture, and I
know Armin from far and wide, he is a really good boy, but we have never thought about marriage until

now, and Mr. Armin is still in the army, so give us a chance. And Armin should finish his military
service in this opportunity so that we can make a wise decision
I was all focused-on Armin, his eyes were following one direction
and his face was expressionless as if
he had noticed the unfortunate incident.
He said nothing to his father, there is no problem, Armin himself
wants to finish his military service
as soon as possible and hopefully we will serve you again, and after
all the words and talks, they left
our house.
Armin and I had become more and more dependent, so much so
that nothing was important to us
except being together
One day when we were walking, he told me that the first day of
fourth month is going to the army
and that he has done all his work...
I knew that doing military service was 90% because of me...
I told him that I will miss you more and he laughed and said that
there is no way, your father made
this a condition for me and I have to go through this stage as well.
After all the talking and walking, Armin went to military service and
I was alone both at work and at
home.
I wasn't in contact with him, which means I couldn't be in contact at
all. After a few weeks of Armin's

military service, another suitor came to our house, and I saw how much my father was prepared for
this proposal, and he came to me and said that my daughter is the son of so-and-so friend...
They are in good financial condition
The same person who works and talks with his father all day in the company
And he was imposing his thoughts and opinions on me.
Until that age, I had not been able to make a decision for myself or disobey the family's decisions,
especially my father's, that's why I shared this story with my mother and told her that I love Armin,
he went to the army because of me so that we can get back together and get married.
My mother had told this to my father, but without paying any attention to what he said, she said
that I know men and I know who is worthy of Shida and who can make her happy.
My whole soul and body were numb, I was in a situation where my decisions and authority were no
longer in my hands, I was like a dead fish in the water, I was motionless...
My father's friend got the yes answer from my father that night and left our house happy. All me
thoughts were with Armin.

He missed me even when I was with him, even though he would never see me with him again

What's going on for Armin?

What will happen to my life?

I went to a room full of girls' toys and put my head on the shoulder of one of them, and my tears

flowed uncontrollably from the corners of my eyes.

Armine's image was in front of my eyes at every moment

And he squeezes my throat until I even let out my breath forcefully

A few days passed; I received a call from an unknown number. It was Armine's voice

A sad and sad voice as if he knows everything...

At first, I beat myself up because I didn't recognize him, but I couldn't talk to him anymore, it was like

separating flesh from bones, my whole soul and heart hurt.

In order to keep him away from me, I didn't tell him anything about the incident because I knew that

if he knew about this matter, he would ruin it and destroy my family and even himself...

And I was even afraid that he would hurt himself

In order to make him hate me, I used to say things that made me hate myself...

I told him that I am already married...

Every day, Armin's love and affection take root in my heart and soul.

To the extent that I no longer had any feelings for my life partner or for life itself...

I finished the whole story a few months ago...

And I saved myself from my father's several-year prison that he had created for me

This is how I valued the rest of my life

And I will spend the rest of my life with Armin's real romances. The pleasure I get in this distance

and pain is much better for me than artificial life and being with someone I don't love.

Shida said her words and at the end of her words, a heavy pain took her throat and she became

silent...

She became silent and I drowned in the sea of feelings and love that was in her...

My breath became heavier and forced out of my lungs

I remembered Armin's shortness of breath at night, which was now as clear as day for me

Armin was the same boy who told me about his girlfriend Shida's betrayal in the military dormitory

that night...

I asked him, do you not know about Armin anymore...

He said why did I hear that a soldier left Iran?

My whole body and soul were shooting, what had happened, it was like I was a vessel and the pains

and sorrows of both sides were dissolved in me, I felt so uncomfortable...
I didn't say anything about Armin to her and I didn't say that he was in the service with me one day...
And I didn't say how much he missed you in the middle of the night in the barracks...
I just said one sentence to her...
That's right!! Love grabs a person's throat somewhere...
And you have no way back and no way forward...
You get stuck between staying and leaving, and in the end, the power of love is much greater than your endurance...
I didn't know where this sentence came to my mind and I said it, but my interpretation of love was always that it comes from nowhere and penetrates to the deepest layer of your heart and takes root in it every day...
It hits you like lightning...
And it takes you back from what you are and leaves you in another world...
It may save you and it may paint you like a hidden pain...
But in the end, whether with his salvation or with the pain he inflicts on your life, he will make you drunk...
He laughs at you with crying eyes...
Until then, I didn't know anything about the characteristics of girls and women...

The only mentality I had about them was that they are very
superficial people and spend their lives
according to the appearances of the things and trivial things....
And they have no understanding and experience of being deep...
And they never like silence...
And even people who are deeply in love are not...
That day, all my beliefs were in danger...
I had seen a girl who after many years still lives in her imagination
with her lost love.
And the boy who takes all his memories leaves his country
That night passed with all its sweetness and bitterness and everyone
went back home and started their own world...
They left and took a part of my existence and feelings with them
It took my friend's childish joy when it was his birthday and he was
excited to bloom like a smiling bud
to the middle of the party in the romantic world of my married
friends and at the end drowning in
the pain of endless mad love....
I lived all of them as if I wasn't created for a specific path and I
didn't have a path for myself
And I always accompanied people and they invited me to their joys
and sorrows and took a part of my soul with them...
I wanted to calm down and get rid of all that thinking about this and
that and get to a state of
being where I enjoy everything and see myself in the mirror
cheerfully and excitedly...

I was tired of life, all its sorrows and joys
From drowning in events to being tired of the respect of those around me.
I reminded myself that he has no romance, no one to listen to his heartache and know what is going on
on in his heart, how lost I felt in the world, no one saw my game?
Little by little, I was reaching the deepest level of loneliness.
I came home late at night and went straight to my bed so that sleep could calm me down a bit
I always had an old notebook next to my pillow where I occasionally wrote down my thoughts
I picked it up and looked at it, my eyes fell on a sentence...
Repeating the sentence that I left in the corner of the blackboard several years ago and I needed it
more than ever.
The birth of the first bird from the cage of my heart:
"One day I will leave this swamp with my whole body and soul...
With the dream of a calm beach, I put my head on the rocks and my heart in the sea.
I whispered this sentence under my lips and fell asleep.
I slept so much that many years of my life had passed, and I had not understood anything, I had spent
my days amidst the useless repetition of life, I was lost in the chaos, I got to know the pains with me
bones, I practiced the laughter of fake. And I learned.

I woke up when I was a tired and listless old man who had nothing to say. My life was busy and
recently it stopped my heart from beating.
One day, unaware of myself, in the middle of the gradual death of my soul and soul, I found myself
inside a solar car that had no driver.
They had installed smart wristbands on my hand, which determined my route
They also hung a small metal piece around my neck that recorded all my words
Wherever and whenever I moved or said something other than the designated framework, the
warnings would be on for me, and my alarm would reach the center of the control body.
Now I had stepped into an era that
Things had become so easy that I had recorded the route to work with my mobile phone and a
driverless car came next to me and picked me up to take me to work.
And while sitting, he greeted me with his robotic voice and wished me a good journey
I had stepped into the year 2083 and most of our life was related to machines and intelligent robots
that had pushed humans further and further away from each other…
There was no feeling inside that car and inside that city for me
At the end of my 85 years, I was going to work

I had become like a tape that the past was vivid in my mind only for the last one year and as time
passed, the events were cleared from the other side of my mind.
Our lives were so routine and controlled that we ourselves gradually forgot that inside us there is a
heart full of love and emotion that beats us.
Everyone was programmed from birth to death
And all the people had their duties specified for them
to wake up at a specific time in the morning and go to sleep at a specific time at night
Every moment of our lives had been determined
that there was no time left to think and love and self-knowledge
Our hearts did not spread the feeling that was inside, that kindness, that smile, that friendship and
that compassion that maybe years ago were in us and kept us alive and gave life.
During the day, perhaps in emergency situations, people would exchange conversations with each
other, and that was only to save the lives of machines and devices that worked for humans.
From zero to one hundred people's lives had become dependent on technology and working with
machines
The streets were so crowded that to get rid of these events, people could take refuge in the deserts

and forests for only a few days during the year to align with nature and their divine nature.
The cars were driverless and self-controlled and without any noise, if you put a glass of water in it,
not a drop of water would drip for hours...
They took us to our destination slowly and comfortably...
Unaware that these comforts in the new era had made humans more like robots and there was no
feeling of joy and happiness in humans.
In the midst of my everyday life, I rarely remember anything from years ago
I rarely remembered the mood of youth, enthusiasm and liberation
One day I was walking in the middle of the road
For a few moments, my thoughts took me back to 65 years ago in a taxi that I always used to go to
school and the people who sat and talked in it. I forgot that the old man went to work every day with
a sack in his hand and he always talked inside the car. Indeed, that old man should not be alive
anymore, maybe one day in the midst of the hardships of that era, he gave up his life and was relieved...
But if he were alive, no one would be sad about unemployment, because at this point in history, grief
had no meaning at all, and no one was unemployed at all, people were completely full all the time, and
there was no time to think and stay idle.

Or, better to say, the feeling of other people's pain was completely forgotten
Everyone was leading their lives in their own self-made world
But now, if that old man was here, he could earn money without working and save himself from the
poverty that plagued him for years. He could get a lot of money for every sentence that comes out of his mouth...
He could be employed somewhere and get paid for the words that he liked from the bottom of his
heart, those sentences full of passion and emotion, something that was rare at this time were real
words full of love and affection, and people paid huge money for him. They were giving, the voice that
came from the bracelet on my hand told me that you have reached your destination and you should get off.
I quickly got out of the car
And in the middle of the line for old men, I walked slowly and with pain in all my body parts
In the middle of the road that brings me to work, I saw a flower bush, I wanted to get closer and
smell it, just like the old habit of communicating with every flower or tree that I saw as if they were
a living being than us, and even for several minutes. I was talking to them; they had life and gave life.
Their perfumes spread in a few meters around them and caressed the feelings and souls of people...

I got close to that bush, closed my eyes and deeply smelled the flower that came out of it, I could not smell any of it, I brought my nose closer and stuck it to the flower and smelled again. It sounded like a warning, I looked down, a small screen was lit under the flower, and the text written inside it was:

Please choose to play your favorite scents:

Rose 2010

Rose of Mohammadi 2020

Lilies

Mixed flowers from the streets of Tehran in 2000

And many old flowers whose names were written there.

I don't think that at that time there will be anyone who wants to pay for smelling those flowers

Humans didn't need to do this at all because they were only looking for their needs at all hours of the day

Daily needs that were formed in their minds

And they did not have any priority in planning the society

I was also lost in these events, but still a bit of my heart was not resolved in it

I bent down

I chose a flower by chance

The option of paying online to spread the smell of that flower became clear to me...

I didn't go to choose the options anymore...

In order to smell the perfume of a flower, you had to pay for it first.

I stood there for a few moments, closed my eyes, and my mind quickly took me to my grandfather's garden in one of the remote villages of the city in ancient times.
I sat next to the rose bush, whose fragrance filled the entire garden, and I drew the combination of the smell of damp earth and roses into my heart and soul, opened my eyes and walked away from there...
In the middle of the way, the thoughts and feelings deposited in my mind and heart passed through my eyes one by one.
From time to time, among the useless beats of my heart, the pulse of love and the feeling of an arrow hit my heart and passed.
I liked to shout in the middle of the crowded streets where people were coming and going, and they were all connected to the city network, and I would explain to them a little bit of the smell of that rose, and make them smile so much that I could see the smile line on their faces, or a few people. I would gather them together and tell them jokes and make them laugh.
But they did not hear my old man's words.
They never heard my words
I knew that even if I told them a joke for hundreds of years, it would not bring a smile to their faces...

Even if they wanted to laugh, they should be placed in special places
where laughing is free, and they
would laugh quietly and that would be it...
In most of the places that I saw, there were billboards saying that it
was forbidden to laugh, it was
forbidden to talk and it was forbidden to stand.
On the way to work, my legs stopped walking.
They were taking their last breaths...
They had tolerated me for 83 years and carried me here and there on
their shoulders...
And I had not once shown kindness to them.
I felt that I could not walk anymore.
Walking into an environment where I did not see any feelings,
smiles or love.
I felt that people's feelings of love, kindness, and affection are like
flesh being separated from my bones
And I must not let this happen
If you take a soul from a soul, take a heart away from love and
affection, and take a human being from
another human being, life will end, and nothing will be given to a
person except living in vain.
What I wanted to do all my life was to be able to bring people closer
together and tell them a story
of empathy and happiness.
I stopped halfway and changed my path
I was moving in a direction where all the warnings,

Warnings...

signs...

And no prohibitive billboards.

My feet were moving in front of me, the same pillars that prevented me from going to my usual work,

now it's as if they are taking refuge somewhere to relieve fatigue.

I moved for several hours, and I gradually reached places where the people did not have any tools or

monitors in their hands. They had handcuffs on me, they loudly informed me of the path I had left. I

turned them off and suffered all the consequences of this.

I was looking at the end of the road

I had reached a point where I preferred death to this life

I stood next to an old tree that was older than me

And I leaned on him

Like me, he may have been carrying a deep sadness

The grief of his lost

The sorrows of those who once talked and laughed loudly in its shadow

And the grief of his old friend, the river.

which always passed by him with joy and enthusiasm

At night, his voice lulls him to sleep.

Now none of them were left for him, he was alone and alone.

And he had heard that in the coming days, to rejuvenate the urban fabric, trees and nature, they have also taken permission to take him and donate his body to print the book "The most modern life in which man has no role".

The only remnant of him was his soul, which was still flying in the highest layer of the sky and thousands of sparrows were singing on its branches and leaves.

Its heart was a refuge for migratory birds

I stood next to him for a few minutes and while I was leaning on him.

I was thinking about the similarities between me and that tree...

The same excited and curious boy 60 years ago who used to be full of smiles in the midst of childish joys...

And he was alive with everyone's laughter

And he used every bit of his being to bring a smile to someone's face, or to help someone, or to keep kindness, affection, and intimacy alive in his heart.

The same person whose whole body and soul was a puzzle of all humans.

To make it complete, you put together smiles, take sorrows and crawl among the greens and plains.

And now there was nothing left of that boy.

He was like a drop of the sea that was full of love, smile and kindness, he was left in the middle of a large volume of water that they made and it did not dissolve. And he never did.

And he still lived in the memory of that sea that was full of love and kindness.

The same sea that could not fit in any container and no world could bind it.

And it did not reach a dead end anywhere around it, and it had all the rivers in it.

His embrace was always open to any river; he was always waiting for the marsh far away from home

I was cut off from that sea.

And that infinity which was the source of salvation for all the trees, greens, thorns and flowers....

Now that drop left from the sea of love had fallen into a self-made container that had been

manipulating his whole soul for years.

A vessel whose water moved in a predetermined direction

He sets fire to the thorns in the distance

And he watered the trees as much as the fruits he picked.

Yes, I was that drop that the boiling sea of love in me still did not leave me alone and pulled me towards him.

Sometimes with a smile

Sometimes by holding the calloused hands of an old man...

And sometimes, successive grudges for the distant drops that were unaware of their origin...

I was returning all of myself to the sea from which I received love and with which my life was filled

with love, flowers and smiles...

And this giving of life was like a seed that I sowed among people, among thorns, flowers, plains, and deserts...

As much as I finished, I sprouted as much....

I put my head on the shoulder of the old tree and closed my eyes. I knew that the soul that is inside that tree, that endless love, even if it turns into paper that destroys the whole soul of that tree, it will still be an eye that will see that love. In the middle of the writings, he will realize the smoothness of the nature of that paper.

I shed tears of love at the foot of that tree and felt the joy of sprouting those drops in my soul

Maybe those tears that I shed will rain one day and blow to the roots of lifeless trees and give them life.

I wrote a few lines of poetry for him...

You are the same old tree that made me aware of my roots with your roots

You survived with love...

I knew that if a drop of that sea of love reached your roots, you could talk about the greatness of that sea in your branches and leaves for years...

Now that you have completed yourself and given branches, fruits and leaves from your being...

It's time to give your life to the papers and everything that will be made of you and plant the seeds

of your hope and kindness on them...
One day, among the lines and marks on your papers, someone will see your smooth and kind heart and
it will grow to your size.
I told him this, I moved away from him...
Endless sense of freedom and liberation embraced me...
I was walking and experiencing flight...
My steps kissed the low and high ground and crossed...
Every now and then I was looking for a lost person who would read me again and sing me in his poems
But I had taken my eyes off the people
I knew that flowers no longer have their own color and smell...
And the leaves of the trees could turn into a color every day and every moment by the choice of humans...
But a wave of life had formed in me, like if you had planted a flower years ago in the middle of
nowhere and you could see its blossoms from afar and look at the smile on your face...
The moments were sweeter and more beautiful for me.
My age and all my fatigue filled me as if I were 83 years old...
I had thrown away all my fears
I had abandoned everything that is good and gone astray
Like that childhood and youth, I drowned among people and I didn't want to accept that they no
longer have feelings of love, affection, and kindness inside them...maybe they did, but the faces and

behaviors and most importantly, life and mixing in societies He had taken them from them now.

I didn't want to see them without a smile

A movement came to my feet and I was looking for an excuse to make them happy or help them.

But in the middle of their smile full of love

May my life and soul be renewed.

I did not see anyone around

I was walking away and my steps were singing a colorful song...

And inside me, a 20-year-old boy was still thinking of helping and bringing a smile to the faces of others.

A rebellious wind had passed through the layers of tall and nested buildings that even water could

not pass through them. He reached around me and as if he had come from far away and brought

souvenirs, he was excited for me.

It had been a long time since I had seen such a fierce and unruly wind.

Unless, among the four designated pieces of wood, in a specific period of time, they produced wind with

advanced devices and showed the movement of objects to the public. And they charged people for

these scenes.

How many times I took a deep breath from that turbulent wind and I knew that it had reached there

from the most distant and uncharted places, and it did not have the
slightest dust or dirt, and there
was nothing to move on the ground. My heart is for the dust that
always rises from those winds. I
could have missed it...
But there was no earth left on the ground and no earth that the wind
could wake up and put on us bodies.
He was carrying only one bag from Goltan Goltan, which at this
time of life was strange to leave
anything on the ground.
Surely the earth's alarmists were asleep when such garbage was
appearing on the street.
That same old black bag that had no name or address left for several
years.
The bag came and came and with the twist that he gave himself, he
got stuck in a bush. The closer I
got, the license plate of the bush, which I read, said the lily bush of
2003.
To release the scent, press the button and put your nose in the
designated place...
Those bushes spread the smell of the flowers written on the license
plate for a few seconds after
receiving the fee...
I drew everything that was left inside my card and put my nose close
to the flower for a few moments
and pressed the play option.

The smell of lotus flower spread for a moment and then it was gone
At that moment, I felt alive and felt the real smell of a flower that took me back many years...
That flower smelled of the swamp in which it lived years ago, and now it had grown out of it, and it had displayed its pleasant smell.
Who knew that flower?
He should have taken his head out of the mud that was holding his feet and stopped his growth and displayed his beauty...
At that moment, I felt the pure smell of the lotus flower, which was from that marsh that wanted to reach the sea and release itself for years.
Now a lotus flower had grown from that pond, which the whole world would have to pay a huge price to smell for a moment.
I breathed all that smell into my soul and body and took that old bag and a souvenir from the era of love and affection from its bush.
I crumpled in my hands and walked away...
I was going farther and farther; I was holding that bag so tightly in my hands that I knew that if a camera saw it in the hand of a person, the alarm would sound and they would immediately take it from me. Those bags were collected and had no place in this day and age. I don't know where and how that

wind brought it to this day and brought it to me...
I held it in my hands with its old memories that were inside and I moved further away from the houses and tall buildings and reached a place where there were more open neighborhoods and smaller houses with higher ceilings...
And there were people from ancient times left among its alleys.
who had given them the right to live in that area?
They had a plate between their wrists that indicated which region they belong to and they should not leave the border that was marked for them, otherwise they would have to pay a heavy price.
And when I came there, I crossed many red lines without getting a ticket.
I had crossed the line between life and death
I was walking in the streets of that area and looking around.
My legs, which had been supporting me for many years and carrying my weight, now seemed to have been abandoned and were moving empty and empty...
I used to see the small holes left from years ago in those alleys and put my feet in them and enjoy it.
In that area where I always went to work and lived, there were no holes in the ground, the entire surface of the ground was made uniform like glass.
That day, I broke all the boundaries that I had created for myself in my mind and reality and stepped into the unknown.

Only because my legs could no longer tolerate me, nor my heartbeat enjoyed its beating.
And I had no patience left in my hands.
I wanted to bring them to a place where they could drink a little water from the fountain of them
originality so that I could move again.
The doors left from the year 2000 were displayed in a showcase, and some visitors who had tickets to
come to that area looked at them with amazement and surprise.
And an explanation about the effectiveness of those cracks was written in ancient times:
With this tool, people moved their things and sometimes put things on it for sale and turned their lives around...
And the photos of several people who gave their lives in this way were pasted above the showcase
My eyes fell on one of those pictures, I narrowed my eyes, I couldn't read his name, but a familiar face caught my eye.
It was Gholam Hossein Garichi's[†] shop where he used to sell fish years ago. The same person who
brought me fish and I used to sell it in a small shop.
The same fish shop that I just understood why it kept away from humans, why it lives in the middle of nature
I became more and more immersed in the real world full of emotions and kindness of that time...

[†] A person who sells things on a rack

I remembered how much I had a life full of excitement and happiness among people and sometimes I was sad about the things that I now miss for my sorrows....
I was moving with a mind full of feelings and love, which was the origin of my heart...
Behind me I heard the sound of a child crying...
I sat down and turned to look and saw that a little girl was crying so much next to her mother that her face was wet with tears.
It had been a few years since I heard a child crying in the crowd, but I understood that
Crying is not prohibited in this area as long as no one has sent a report of crying to the information center and has not filed a complaint.
Something new and strange...
All the children are under the supervision of special teachers who bring them in a pasteurized and linear form
Among the thousands of children in the society, few of them cried and they considered crying as an illness and they dealt with it...
From the very beginning of infancy, the children were carried linearly and with a certain rhythm.
It's like there was only one dimension in their lives, like a coin that has only one side and when you throw it in the air, you're sure what will come up.

They really set a fence for us from the very beginning so that you don't get out of it and realize your own authority and power...
But this was a disaster for children and humans. Humans, especially children at a young age, must be made and formed from the sadness, joy, sweetness and bitterness of reaching and not reaching, and understand all aspects of life by themselves.
I got closer to them and sharpened my ears a little to hear their words...
The little girl was repeating the word fish, fish among her cries....
And she asked his mother for fish... her mother, without paying attention to her child's words, was only trying to muffle her voice so that no one would be upset...
When she saw me, he was more afraid that I might cause trouble for them.
I stood next to them and looked at that little girl with a smile
Her free cries bring a smile of liberation to my lips...
On the other side, the crying of a girl without limits, and on the other side, the smile of an old man who had not seen a smile on his lips for years.
Undoubtedly, the sweetest cry that invited me to happiness and freedom was the cry of that little girl
When I looked at her a little, she raised her small hand and was pointing to the far side with her finger, and her eyes were asking me for fish... I want those fish...

Her mother did not pay any attention to me or the child and only looked at our wordless communication.

My heart beat faster as if you have been thirsty to help someone for years and now the chance had come.

At that age, like a child, I went towards that little girl's index finger.

Her cries had given me life.

And making her little wish come true was now my only happiness at that moment...

And seeing the clear sky in her eyes after all the rain was like a rebirth for me

I moved a few meters away and told her to stay there to bring you fish.

A few hundred meters away from that little girl, colorful fish were placed on a busy street corner.

Each in its own packaging...

I stood there for a while; I had no money to buy fish

All that was in my service card, I carried behind me to smell the smell of lotus flowers.

People were passing by me and each of them looked at me in a strange way.

I didn't have any license plate or identification, and since I was not from that area, I had entered

that area from somewhere else without knowing, and I felt strange.

How can I get one of those fish for that girl??

My whole being was filled with excitement and fear along with heart palpitations

I had lowered my head and kept myself from the eyes of people.
I was unknown there, no one knew me, just because I didn't have
the sign and license plate of people in that area.
No one understood my inner feeling at that time.
I had been used to being misunderstood for a long time and I didn't
consider anyone watching over my work.
I moved slowly and when I passed by the shop, I picked up one of
the fish that was in the basket and
moved on, neither looking inside the shop nor looking at any of the
people around me.
When I picked up the fish, I felt fear all over me. I opened the
crumpled black bag in my hand and
dropped the fish in it and held it tightly. You will sentence me to a
year of loneliness
Half a year to harvest fish
And half a year of entering an area where I had not paid a ticket or
fee to enter
But at that moment, my heart was finding the beats of the previous
years.
I wanted that day to be the last day of my life
And then I didn't think about anything.
I had put all the wishes of that girl in that black bag and I was going
towards her and I knew she
was waiting for me.
I needed the taste of that little girl's smile after catching that fish to
survive.

I was a few steps away when I heard a loud voice behind me.

I froze for a moment and my whole body got cold

It is as if you cause the death of a person in one scene and everyone is thirsty to kill you

My death at that moment was not a strange thing at all. I had literally spent several years of me

life with a gradual death

The only thing that hurt me was not being able to see the smiles of that waiting child

I realized that the owner of the shop saw me while I was taking the fish and followed me to take it

from me.

I had nothing to say, I had done something wrong, which is considered against the established law

The voice of the fishmonger behind me got louder and louder. My ears were completely blocked as if

they were blown and I couldn't hear any sound anymore.

My head was down and I was holding the bag tightly with my hands and every now and then I looked

at the little girl who I couldn't tell from a distance if she was happy or still crying.

I took a few steps towards her, but one moment someone grabbed my shirt from behind and pulled me.

This thief came here from another area, his license plate does not belong to this area at all

Report this immediately

Someone said take this to the security inspector...
Someone from the other side said that he is at the end of his life,
take him to work in the corner of
the workshop until he is done...
He took the bag from my hand and took the fish and pushed me to
my side.
It's as if they pulled the cord of happiness from me.
I'm empty...
No one was alive in me anymore.
My hands were empty.
I considered myself finished, someone who will never experience
any love again and all the joys inside
and in his heart were buried.
I had no way back and no way forward.
I knew that day would be the day of my sad death
And I was no longer hanging on to any hope
I had not been able to deliver that fish to the girl, nor that black bag
that had brought me longstanding
wishes.
They took both of them from me and I moved towards the alley
empty-handed.
I didn't know what I would say to the girl, maybe if I was in front of
her, I would have knelt next to
her and cried, and I would have screamed in a sad voice about the
black bag and the wishes that were
taken from me.

Does that mean no one was paying attention to me?
That is, no one among all these people could see that feeling and that inside of me.
There was no one to defend me, the old man.
So where was God?
Where is the God who has seen my whole story from the beginning of my life to the end?
When will it arrive?
He brought me to end the story of my life like this;
My hope was taken away from people and I thought that the end of the story of kindness and feeling
and love is here
And I have finished my affections and kindnesses and I will not get any pleasure and it is time to go
I was born to sympathize, to help, to sprout and grow in humans.
My roots were among the hearts of those whose lips I had brought a smile to.
I approached the alley; the girl and her mother had left there.
Maybe they had seen me from afar and understood that they had taken all their wishes from me and
that I could not do anything for them.
I passed by the side of the alley and entered a quiet walk so that no one would notice me.
I caught myself from the onslaught of words, hatred and anger that was in the eyes and inside of
people and I turned to a lonely alley.

I raised my head and was moving like a calm boat left on the sea.
My hands were empty and my heart was still beating hard because of the laughter of that girl.
I was a few steps away from the people and I picked myself up and was walking forcefully when I felt
an aura of energy and heat behind me as if I was standing near a fire.
I felt that a mountain of people lined up behind me and their breath warmed me and stopped me from
leaving.
My legs stopped going
I could feel that someone is coming behind me and wants to swallow my whole being and release the
bonds that were woven around my heart, soul and body and leave me like a dove in the boundless sky, I
felt that there is someone in He watched my story behind me like a movie and now he wants to hug me.
I didn't know if these thoughts that were going through my head were imaginary or real, but I
wanted not to miss that moment and consider it real.
I stood up and wanted to turn my head and see what we see in my dreams.
I turned my head and saw a young boy standing a few meters away from me
His hands were shaking from stress, his eyes were full of anger and he stood firmly in his place.
He had green eyes and slightly blond hair.

It was as if he wanted to hug me with all the sadness, excitement
and anger that was in him.
And he gave me all his sorrows at that moment and calmed down...
I was looking at him as if he
understood my whole story and wanted to help me. He was standing
in front of me.
Like an incredible dream, I saw all that kindness next to me
The silence of his voice was not like other voices for me, my ears
heard a muffled scream in his voice
Not only my ears but also my body
but the ear of my heart and feelings
that boy
It was a mixture of greed and malice and kindness
Greed and malice and kindness.
Our eyes were locked, I was looking at him more calmly, but he was
embracing me with his eyes like 60
years ago, and saying that I have understood all of you, I have seen
the whole story of your life, all the
kindness in your heart. I have felt and now I have been sent to you
from the endless sea for a
distant drop to be you so that you know that this is not the end of
the story and you are not alone.
To throw all your sufferings, your wholeness, your whole inside,
which was full of love and affection,
into the sea.

At that moment, I felt that a whole world got to know me and that I am no longer a stranger, and
now the seed that I had planted years ago in the middle of nowhere is now drinking water from the
sea of love and blossoming.
As our eyes were talking to each other, there was a smile of satisfaction on my lips... and that young
boy was full of compassion and love. At that moment, I felt that someone from me exists in this life
and this world. He makes me breathe and he has seen all my movies, now he came to me to continue my role
He was the same person, the same seed that I had planted many years ago, now he wanted to make me blossom
His youth was so full of love and kindness and feelings that my whole body and soul was filled with an
aura of light and warmth, and for the first time I saw and felt God by my side with all my heart.
I realized that he saw me every moment and answered all my actions.
He never leaves a drop that falls away from the infinite sea of his grace and mercy and always leaves
a way for you to return to its safe embrace.
Sometimes with a tree...
sometimes with the cry of a girl...
Sometimes with a wind that calms your soul.

In that moment of my life, I was dissolved in the sea of God's love, and for a moment my whole body
and soul were dissolved.
Indeed, today's world is full of robots, machines and routine lives
He needed someone like that young boy
Someone who speaks of kindness and love even if he doesn't have a voice.
Someone like him, who when his kind gets upset or a problem happens to him, tries his best to do something for him...
Someone who sows a seed of love and affection everywhere in this land with every step and keeps his
feelings and heart alive forever.
Without opening my mouth to that young boy, we talked a lot, and I returned, calm and happy, took my way, and left.
There is someone from me in this world who cares about human suffering.
And it doesn't pass by the events and humanity indifferently.
I was flowing like a river and I knew that the end of this river is the boundless sea of God's grace and love
The sea where all the rivers will rest one day...
And again, they will reach the lifeless roots of trees and people and will make life green and give life.
I moved away from there, the peace and love of God took over my entire being
After what happened to me, a new birth was formed in me. I realized that I had been away from the

path of love and kindness for years and I realized that my soul was squeezed and hurt in the hands of a soulless life.

I left and never returned to the previous place of my life

I left everything I had in the past, all the ties that were tied to my body and soul

And the society had raised me like a robot to keep that light of love and divinity off in me

I built a house for myself in the middle of a small farm, every part of it was full of love and life for me,

I planted many flowers and trees there.

And I wanted only one thing from God, between this house and the garden that I have made for

myself, and my moments were spent in happiness and gratitude.

And that desire was to see again the young boy who saved me from the death of my feelings and

emotions and gave me life.

And I had so much faith in God that I knew that one day in the middle of the events of life, your path

will lead you from here to hear my story and take that path full of love and feeling of God and leave a

footprint of goodness and kindness from yourself instead. put

I told you my story and now there is nothing to worry about and I know that there is an endless love

flowing inside you that can give life and bring people together.

And finally, I will always have one wish with me in my soul, and that is to make all the people of the world happy on a special day.

To know that there is no sadness anywhere in the world on that day and all people are happy.

The old man told his whole story, slowly closed his eyes and fell into a deep sleep.

He slept and woke me up

To know the way and path of my life and to know that everything that comes in my way is a part of

me and in order to be complete I have to give them my soul and give them love.

The same love that God has placed inside us without account.

I realized that I had taken the wrong path of life unconsciously and that's why the love, emotion and

happiness had subsided inside me.

He taught me that in every step we take, we can plant a seed of love, hope, and kindness.

He described me to myself and buried his head among the bushes...

Now it was me and the me who knew me

Yes, I was the whole story

All that story you read...

That blond boy with colored eyes who spent his whole day thinking about putting a smile on the lips of

others to make his heart happy and feed his soul and feelings.

And that foul-mouthed fishmonger who would not let even a Riyal be deducted from his account to

protect his power and money was me...

Even that old thief who knocks himself into every door to make happy the heart of a girl who's whole desire was a fish...
All those people who stood in my way were myself and every time I met a part of myself along the way.
In the path that I had taken, I sometimes went downhill and had enthusiasm, and sometimes I was on a path that I was stuck on for days.
Sometimes on a smooth path, the sound of my movement left a sweet music, and sometimes I was trapped in the pits of the road for days and a sad song was formed in my soul.
Sometimes in the middle of the road, I would blow on the flowers, and sometimes I would despair of going under the taunts of the marshes.
In this journey of time, every event that has happened to me has brought me closer to myself and taken me to the inner layers to keep alive even a drop of feeling and kindness that comes from the infinite sea of God inside everyone. We have to try.
And to find my heartbeats and not ignore my feelings.
At that moment, there was no one left in me except myself, who also rested beside me
And an endless love from God's endless sea flowed inside me, I said to myself:

Anywhere in this world, if you give someone a smile one day, you have given that smile to yourself first
and to others.
Someone will return that smile to you one day in a place you don't even think about
If we hold a hand, that hand and that human being is a part of our being, and in order to stand up, all
people must join hands so that the puzzle of humanity, kindness and love can be put together in a
complete way, and we too can create a beautiful and beautiful plan of ourselves. let's leave
In the entirety of this puzzle, no piece is superior to the other, and all of them are put together to
show a certain content, to announce a unity.
You who are reading this are a part of me, and the hands that write this are your hands, and I tried
to give you all of myself so that you know that your hands are not empty, my hands have written for
you day and night, and the words are written in pen and flowing paper. They have done it so that you
can reach it to your soul with your eyes and be free and find the beats of your kind heart and be full
of love and kindness.
until the day comes
Let's sail together with a heartwarming song and give life to every dried root on the way of life.

May our meeting in the boundless sea be sweet.

I loved you before I was gone and I will love you after I was gone...

And I know that at this moment, the only thing I have access to is loving you.

And here I have a request from you and from myself as well...

Deliver the black bag of wishes to little girls and boys.

Plant a seed of love, kindness and humanity in the hearts of people and don't let the pulse of

humanity, friendship and love fail.

And it will be replaced by smart machines and trained humans and robots

Children's hearts are the roots of us humans

No matter how much love and kindness we inject into those roots, they will give us fruitful and stable trees

Let us know that bringing out a small desire from childhood will polish our soul and body.

And we need them for a beautiful future full of goodness

Since I was a child, I heard that when a plane crashes, they look for its black box to discover all the information inside.

and find the reason for its fall

But here the problem is human.

Fallen humans.

in themselves and inside them and we have to look for the black box of their desires and discover them.

Let's clean the dust from their hearts and replace it with a curtain of kindness and friendship.

The fall of each human being will be painful for each one of us,
whether we know and feel it or
whether we continue unknowingly.
Therefore, we should always embrace each other with love and
kindness, and what happiness is higher
for us than to see a child happy and to make an old man fulfill the
desires of his heart, both of which
are our own.
I love you all
Morteza....

Final heartache:

In the midst of a large amount of technology and the progress of societies and the transformation of
the tempo of lives and cultures, as well as the virtualization of most of the work and lives, many of
the problems of today's human age have been improved and repaired almost by the physical presence
of humans to perform Many jobs have disappeared or become less and less.
It is acceptable that the mechanization of lives and work has been very effective in the process of
urban growth and development and even the progress of societies in terms of industry and
technology and equipment updating and has been involved as much as possible in the comfort of
human affairs today...
but if
Let's look a little inside ourselves and our hearts, which is the source of peace for every human being
and the prosperity of love, affection and empathy in societies. A source originates and the essence of
our hearts from the boundless sea of love that feeds on the spread of love, affection, friendship,
enthusiasm and happiness, which has not been able to be paralleled by today's societies to cause the

prosperity of people and society in terms of spirituality, emotion and humanity. be...
There are other angles here that if we pay a little attention, we will see that our feelings for doing
things or events that happen around us have subsided and there is no enthusiasm left in doing
things or events inside us, we communicate less with each other., and most of our relationship is with
machines and technology, we are less happy by making each other happy and we spend less time to be
kind and loving to each other, our heart rate does not increase for each other or it is better to say
that we have become more indifferent towards ourselves and those around us. Here, technology and
robots will not reach us anymore; this is the place where we should hear the voice of our hearts...
All of us have come together on this earth from one type of creatures called human beings...
And all our fellows, from small to large, from black to white, and from the good or bad of the contract
created between us, we complete a puzzle.
And when this big piece of the puzzle, which is our oneness and unity, will be complete, when we
strengthen that desire to connect to the whole, which has been instilled in us since eternity, and we

consider each other as a part of that unity puzzle, and this is certain and assured. Let's know that if
a small member of the people of the world faces a problem in joining that puzzle, all of us will be
incomplete and we will not experience the full beauty and perfection of love and the puzzle of
humanity and unity, which is the mission of each and every one of us human beings...
In the meantime, as much as possible, we should consider the home of our heart as a safe haven for
fellow humans, and tune the rhythm of our hearts with the happiness and love of others, and also take
a path full of love and kindness, which is the origin of our existence. Let's draw feelings, love and
intimacy to people and today's facilities and technology.

Milton Keynes UK
Ingram Content Group UK Ltd.
UKHW021930080824
446615UK00014B/519